THE
PICTURE
ATLAS
OF THE WORLD

Illustrated by Brian Delf

DORLING KINDERSLEY
LONDON · NEW YORK · STUTTGART

A DORLING KINDERSLEY BOOK

Text by Richard Kemp

Art Editor Lester Cheeseman
Designer Marcus James
Project Editor Susan Peach
Senior Editor Emma Johnson
Consultant Keith Lye
Production Teresa Solomon
Art Director Roger Priddy

First published in Great Britain in 1991
by Dorling Kindersley Limited,
9 Henrietta Street, London WC2E 8PS
Reprinted with revisions 1991
Second edition 1992
Second edition reprinted with revisions 1993 (twice),
1994 (twice), 1995 (twice)

Copyright © 1991, 1992 Dorling Kindersley Limited, London

A CIP catalogue record for this book is available from the British Library

ISBN 0-7513-5358-2

Reproduced in Hong Kong by Bright Arts
Printed and bound in Italy by New Interlitho, Milan

CONTENTS

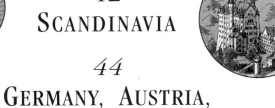

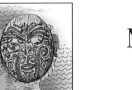

OUR PLANET EARTH

THE EARTH on which we live is one of a family of nine planets which circle around a star called the Sun. The Sun is just one of about 100,000 million stars in our galaxy. On a clear night you can see some of the other stars in the galaxy as a glow in the sky, called the Milky Way. Astronomers estimate that there may be as many as 10,000 million galaxies, which together make up the universe.

THE ATMOSPHERE

The atmosphere is a layer of gases surrounding the Earth. It is about 1,000 km (621 miles) thick and is made of nitrogen, oxygen, carbon dioxide, water vapour, and small amounts of other gases. The atmosphere acts as a protective shield, absorbing much of the heat that reaches the Earth from the Sun. Without it, our whole planet would be burnt to a desert.

Most of the gases in the atmosphere are concentrated in the lowest part, which is called the troposphere. Above this is the stratosphere. This contains the ozone layer, which absorbs harmful ultra-violet rays from the Sun. Above the stratosphere are the mesosphere and the thermosphere. Here the gases are so thin that there is little difference between these parts of the atmosphere and space.

THE SOLAR SYSTEM

The Sun is much bigger than the planets. It has a diameter of about 1,392,000 km (864,948 miles). The diameter of the Earth at the Equator is only 12,714 km (7,747 miles).

The distance from the Sun to the Earth is about 150 million km (93 million miles). If a train left Earth at a speed of 175 kph (110 mph), it would take 96 years to reach the Sun.

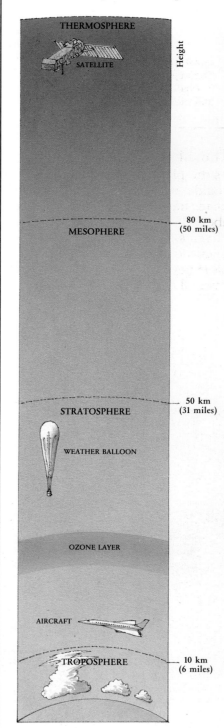

THE EARTH'S SHIELD

The Earth is like a giant magnet. It has two magnetic poles, which lie near the North and South Poles. The Earth's magnetism is probably caused by movement of the molten metals in its outer core. Around the Earth is a region called the magnetosphere, which acts as a huge shield. It protects the Earth from the solar wind, a stream of electrically charged particles from the Sun. Particles that get through the magnetosphere are trapped in the Van Allen belts.

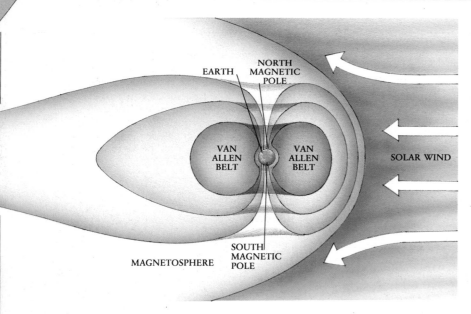

THE SEASONS AND DAYS

It takes a year for the Earth to circle the Sun. The Earth is slightly tilted, so one half of the globe, or hemisphere, is closer to the Sun than the other. This tilt causes the seasons. The hemisphere tilted towards the Sun receives more heat, and so has summer, while the hemisphere that is tilted away has winter. As it circles the Sun, the Earth also spins on its axis, turning once every 24 hours. This rotation causes our days and nights. The side of the Earth facing the Sun has day, while the other side has night.

MARCH
Spring in the northern hemisphere.

DECEMBER
Summer in the southern hemisphere.

MOON

SUN

JUNE
Summer in the northern hemisphere.

SEPTEMBER
Spring in the southern hemisphere.

INSIDE THE EARTH

Scientists believe that the Earth was formed about 4,600 million years ago from a spinning cloud of gas and dust, which shrank to form a hot ball of liquid, or molten, rock. As it cooled, the Earth's surface formed into a solid crust. Under the surface the temperature is so high that parts of the Earth are still liquid. Movement of this molten material in the outer core is thought to produce the Earth's magnetic fields.

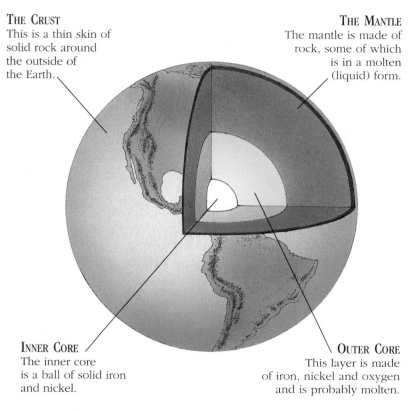

THE CRUST
This is a thin skin of solid rock around the outside of the Earth.

THE MANTLE
The mantle is made of rock, some of which is in a molten (liquid) form.

INNER CORE
The inner core is a ball of solid iron and nickel.

OUTER CORE
This layer is made of iron, nickel and oxygen and is probably molten.

THE WANDERING CONTINENTS

The Earth's crust is made up of pieces called plates, which float on top of a layer of molten rock in the mantle. There are seven main plates and several smaller ones. The magnetic forces within the Earth move the plates slowly around the globe in an ever-changing jigsaw.

Geologists believe that about 270 million years ago all the land on Earth was joined together in one "super-continent", which they call Pangaea. But, as the plates moved around, the land in this super-continent slowly started to split up. This movement is called continental drift. The maps below show how geologists think the continents have moved and split apart to form the landmasses that we know today.

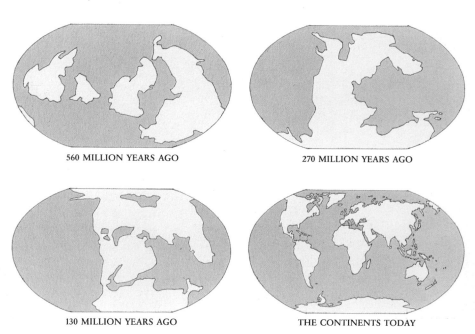

560 MILLION YEARS AGO

270 MILLION YEARS AGO

130 MILLION YEARS AGO

THE CONTINENTS TODAY

THE RESTLESS EARTH

As the plates move around the globe they collide, overlap, and slide past each other. The plates travel very slowly – their fastest speed is about 15 cm (6 in) in a year – but over millions of years the results of this movement can be dramatic. Huge mountain ranges, spectacular rift valleys, and deep trenches in the ocean bed have all been formed in areas where two plates

meet. Earthquakes, volcanoes, geysers and hot mud pools are also caused by plate movements. The regions in the world where they are found closely follow the joins between the plates.

SLIDING PAST
The San Andreas Fault in California is an example of a place where two plates are sliding past each other. The sliding movement often occurs in short bursts which are felt on the surface as earthquakes.

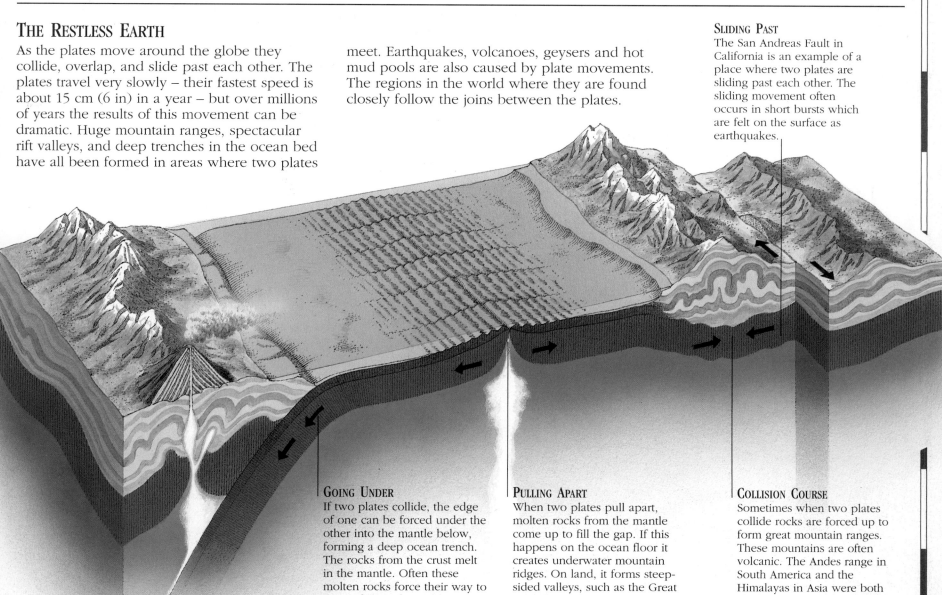

GOING UNDER
If two plates collide, the edge of one can be forced under the other into the mantle below, forming a deep ocean trench. The rocks from the crust melt in the mantle. Often these molten rocks force their way to the surface to form volcanoes.

PULLING APART
When two plates pull apart, molten rocks from the mantle come up to fill the gap. If this happens on the ocean floor it creates underwater mountain ridges. On land, it forms steep-sided valleys, such as the Great Rift Valley in East Africa.

COLLISION COURSE
Sometimes when two plates collide rocks are forced up to form great mountain ranges. These mountains are often volcanic. The Andes range in South America and the Himalayas in Asia were both formed by colliding plates.

CLIMATES AROUND THE WORLD

CLIMATE is the name given to the typical weather conditions and temperature in a particular area. Similar types of climate are found in different places around the world. For example, there are regions of hot, dry desert in Africa, North America, and central Australia.

The climate in any particular place depends partly on its latitude, that is, how far north or south of the Equator it lies. The regions around the Equator are the hottest places in the world. The further away from the Equator you go, the colder the climate becomes. The coldest places in the world are the polar regions around the North and South Poles.

Climate is also affected by how close a place is to the sea. The sea warms and cools the land near it, so coastal areas usually have fewer extremes of temperature than places in the centre of a continent. Another important influence is altitude – how high a place is above sea level. The higher the place, the colder is its climate.

POLAR AND TUNDRA REGIONS
The areas round the North and South Poles are covered in ice. The temperature only rises above freezing point for a few months of the year. South of the North Pole lie regions known as the tundra, where the lower parts of the soil are permanently frozen and only mosses and lichens can grow. As the climate is very dry, the tundra regions are sometimes described as cold deserts.

During the short summer period, the edges of the polar ice caps melt. Large pieces of ice break off and form icebergs.

MOUNTAIN REGIONS
The temperature in mountainous regions varies a lot – the higher up you go, the colder it becomes. Trees and plants often grow on the lower slopes of mountains, but above a certain height (known as the tree line), temperatures are too low for vegetation to survive. Still higher up is the snow line. Above this it is so cold that the ground is permanently covered by snow and ice.

Kilimanjaro in Tanzania lies almost on the Equator, but it is so high that its peak is covered in snow all year round.

TAIGA
Taiga is a Russian word which means "cold forest". It is used to describe the huge areas of evergreen forest that stretch across northern parts of Canada, Scandinavia, and the Russian Federation. Evergreen trees, such as spruces, pines and firs, are the only type of vegetation that can survive in the long, snowy winters and short summers of this type of climate.

The trees in the taiga regions are an important source of wealth. They are used for timber and for making paper.

TEMPERATE FOREST
Much of northern Europe and parts of North America have a temperate climate, which means that the temperature is never very hot or very cold. Because these regions have rainfall throughout the year, they were once covered by forests. Most of these have now been cut down. Deciduous trees, which shed their leaves in the winter, are common in temperate regions.

Much of the land in northern Europe has been cleared for farming, and small pockets of trees are all that is left of the forests.

THE OCEAN FLOOR
The ocean floor is not flat. Like the land, it has many geographical features, such as mountain ranges, flat plains and deep trenches. The longest range of mountains in the world is the underwater Indian Ocean–Pacific Ocean Cordillera. It stretches from East Africa, through the Indian Ocean, round southern Australia, and across the Pacific Ocean to the Gulf of California – a distance of 30,900 km (19,200 miles). The deepest point in the oceans, the Mariana trench in the Pacific Ocean near Japan, is about 11,034 m (36,201 ft) below sea level – deeper than the height of Mount Everest. The shallowest parts of the oceans are the areas of seabed around the edges of the continents, which are called the continental shelves.

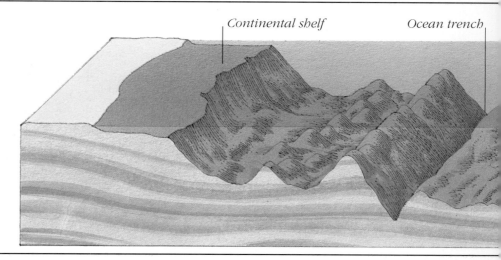

Continental shelf   Ocean trench

MEDITERRANEAN

The name "Mediterranean" is given to the type of climate which is found around the Mediterranean Sea, and in other similar regions of the world, such as California in North America. These areas have hot, dry summers and cool, wet winters. The trees and plants that grow there are specially adapted to survive the lack of water in summer.

Olive trees are one of the few plants that thrive in this climate. They have been cultivated around the Mediterranean for many centuries.

DRY GRASSLAND

In the middle of some of the continents are huge plains of grassland, such as the North American Prairies, the Asian Steppe, and the Argentinian Pampas. These regions have extreme climates – very hot summers and very cold winters. Large parts of these areas have now been taken over for farming and are used for growing wheat or raising cattle.

South American farmers raise large numbers of beef cattle on the grassy plains of the Pampas.

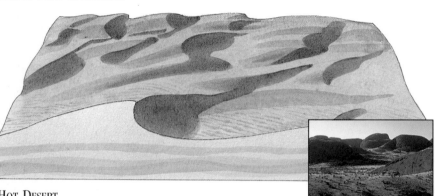

HOT DESERT

The hottest and driest climates in the world are found in the tropical deserts, such as the Sahara in Africa and the Australian Outback. The temperature there often reaches 38° C (100° F) in the shade. In some desert areas there may be no rain for several years. Deserts often contain sandy soil that can only support plants such as cacti, which are adapted to the dry conditions.

The dry, desert plains of the Australian Outback cover more than two-thirds of the continent. Few plants and animals can survive there.

TROPICAL GRASSLAND

Between the wet equatorial rainforests and the hot dry deserts lie regions of tropical grassland, such as the African Savannah. Here the climate is always hot, but the year divides between a dry and a wet season. Tall grasses and low trees and bushes grow in these areas. Tropical grasslands are grazed by large herds of plant-eating animals.

The African Savannah is the last place on Earth where huge herds of grazing animals, such as zebra, gazelles, and wildebeest, still survive.

EQUATORIAL RAINFOREST

In the regions around the Equator, the climate is hot and wet all year round. The temperature remains constant at about 27–28° C (80–82° F). Vegetation thrives in this type of climate, and the equatorial regions used to be covered in dense rainforest. Much of this has now been cut down, although large areas still remain in the Amazon river basin in South America.

The Amazon rainforest covers an area 12 times the size of France. It is home to more species of birds and animals than anywhere else on Earth.

WHERE CLIMATES ARE FOUND

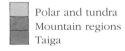 Polar and tundra
 Mountain regions
Taiga

Temperate forest
Mediterranean
Dry grassland

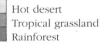 Hot desert
Tropical grassland
Rainforest

Mid-ocean ridge

Volcanic island

THE COUNTRIES OF THE WORLD

ALL OF THE CONTINENTS except Antarctica are divided into different countries, and these vary in size. By far the largest country in the world is the Russian Federation, which stretches across two continents – Europe and Asia. The second largest country is Canada and the third largest is China. At the other end of the scale, the smallest country is the Vatican City, which lies in the city of Rome in Italy. It has a total area of only 0.44 sq km (0.17 sq mile). The Russian Federation is almost 39 million times bigger than the Vatican City.

LATITUDE AND LONGITUDE

To help locate places in the world, geographers draw imaginary lines around the globe. Lines of latitude circle the globe from east to west. They are measured in degrees north or south of the Equator. Lines of longitude circle the Earth from north to south and are measured in degrees east or west of the line called the Prime Meridian.

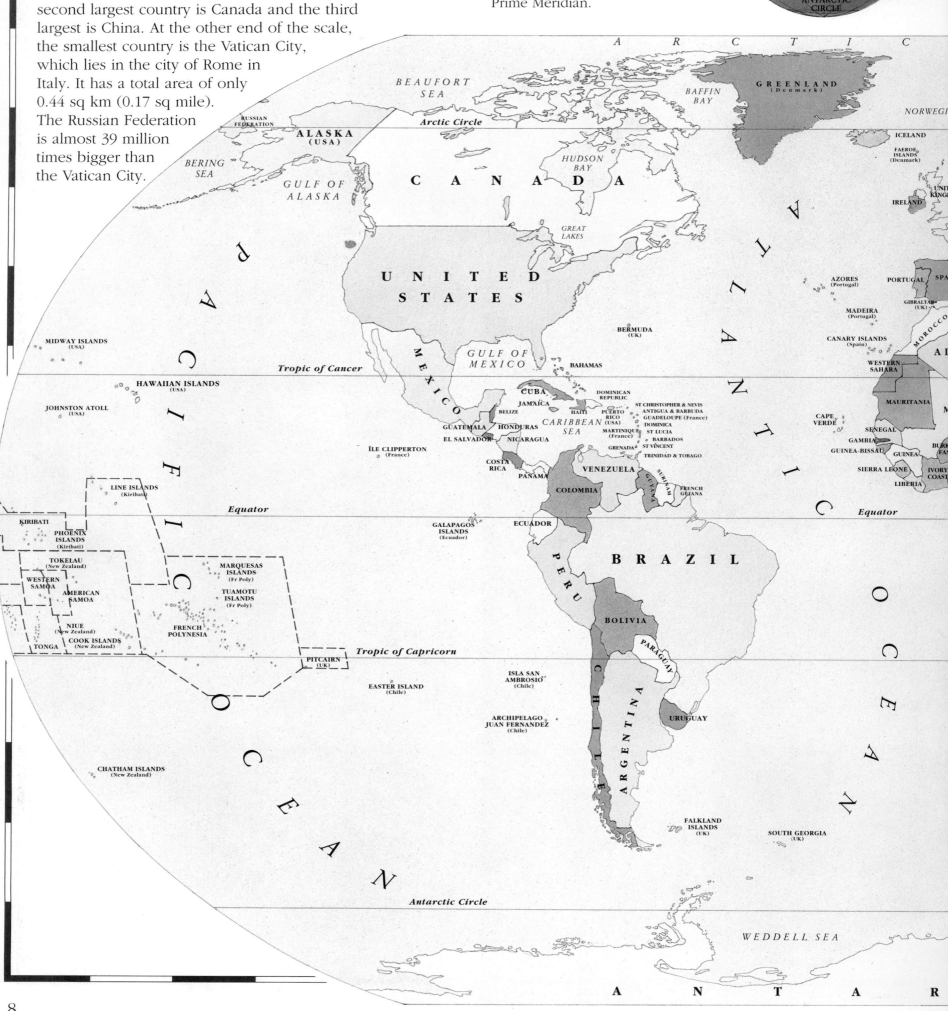

ARCTIC

BEAUFORT SEA

RUSSIAN FEDERATION

Arctic Circle

ALASKA (USA)

BERING SEA

GULF OF ALASKA

PACIFIC

BAFFIN BAY

GREENLAND (Denmark)

NORWEGIA

ICELAND

FAEROE ISLANDS (Denmark)

HUDSON BAY

C A N A D A

GREAT LAKES

U N I T E D S T A T E S

UNITED KINGD

IRELAND

ATLANTIC

AZORES (Portugal)

PORTUGAL

SPAI

MADEIRA (Portugal)

GIBRALTAR (UK)

MIDWAY ISLANDS (USA)

Tropic of Cancer

HAWAIIAN ISLANDS (USA)

JOHNSTON ATOLL (USA)

MEXICO

BERMUDA (UK)

GULF OF MEXICO

BAHAMAS

CANARY ISLANDS (Spain)

MOROCCO

AL

WESTERN SAHARA

CUBA

JAMAICA

HAITI

DOMINICAN REPUBLIC

PUERTO RICO (USA)

CARIBBEAN SEA

MAURITANIA

M

CAPE VERDE

BELIZE

GUATEMALA

EL SALVADOR

HONDURAS

NICARAGUA

ST CHRISTOPHER & NEVIS
ANTIGUA & BARBUDA
GUADELOUPE (France)
DOMINICA
ST LUCIA
MARTINIQUE (France)
BARBADOS
ST VINCENT
GRENADA
TRINIDAD & TOBAGO

SENEGAL

GAMBIA

GUINEA-BISSAU

GUINEA

BURKI
FAS

SIERRA LEONE

IVORY COAST

ÎLE CLIPPERTON (France)

COSTA RICA

PANAMA

VENEZUELA

GUYANA

SURINAM

FRENCH GUIANA

COLOMBIA

LIBERIA

LINE ISLANDS (Kiribati)

Equator

Equator

KIRIBATI

PHOENIX ISLANDS (Kiribati)

GALAPAGOS ISLANDS (Ecuador)

ECUADOR

TOKELAU (New Zealand)

WESTERN SAMOA

AMERICAN SAMOA

MARQUESAS ISLANDS (Fr Poly)

TUAMOTU ISLANDS (Fr Poly)

PERU

B R A Z I L

NIUE (New Zealand)

TONGA

COOK ISLANDS (New Zealand)

FRENCH POLYNESIA

BOLIVIA

PITCAIRN (UK)

Tropic of Capricorn

PARAGUAY

ISLA SAN AMBROSIO (Chile)

EASTER ISLAND (Chile)

C H I L E

ARGENTINA

URUGUAY

ARCHIPELAGO JUAN FERNANDEZ (Chile)

CHATHAM ISLANDS (New Zealand)

OCEAN

FALKLAND ISLANDS (UK)

SOUTH GEORGIA (UK)

Antarctic Circle

WEDDELL SEA

A N T A R R

PACIFIC OCEAN

ATLANTIC OCEAN

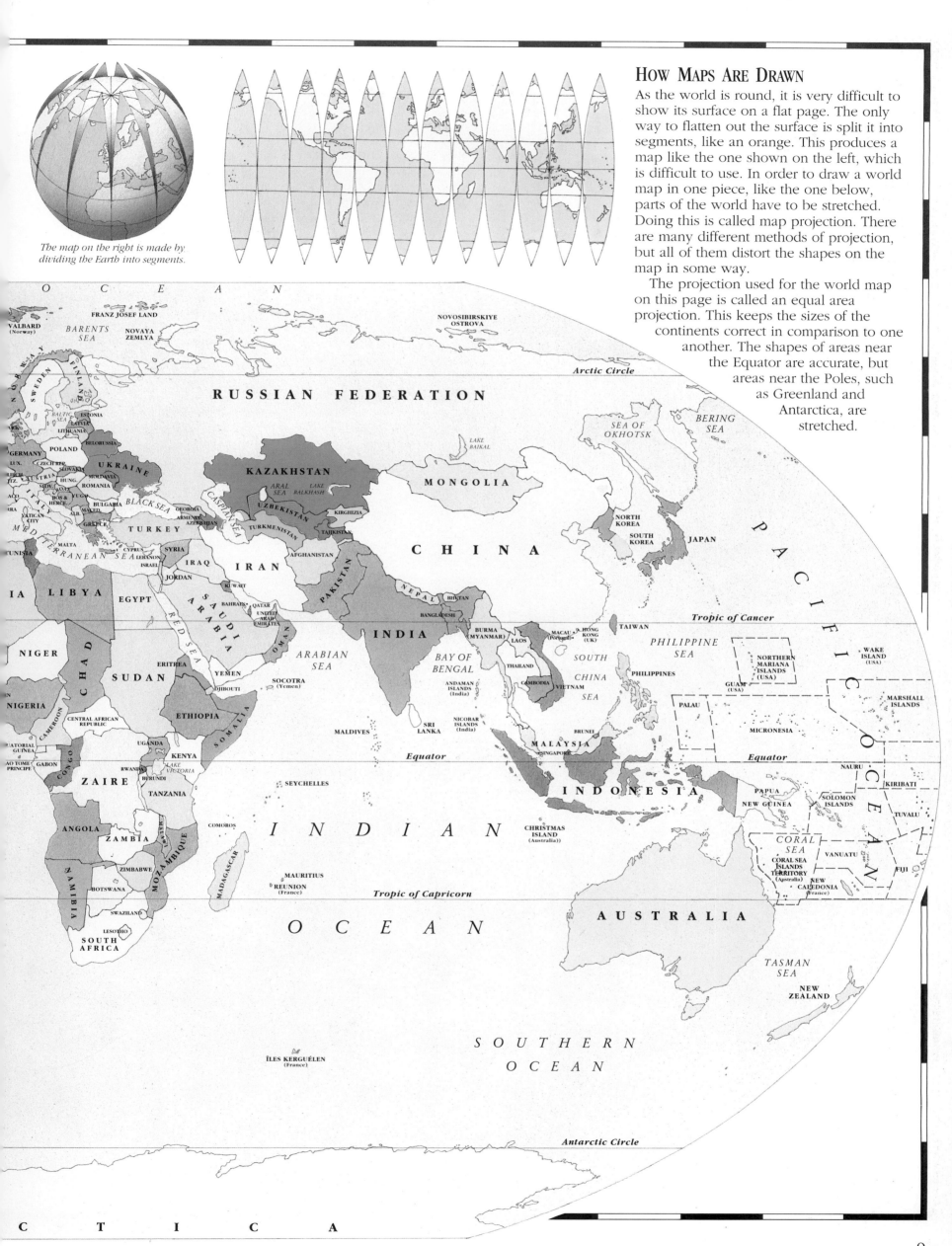

The map on the right is made by dividing the Earth into segments.

HOW MAPS ARE DRAWN

As the world is round, it is very difficult to show its surface on a flat page. The only way to flatten out the surface is split it into segments, like an orange. This produces a map like the one shown on the left, which is difficult to use. In order to draw a world map in one piece, like the one below, parts of the world have to be stretched. Doing this is called map projection. There are many different methods of projection, but all of them distort the shapes on the map in some way.

The projection used for the world map on this page is called an equal area projection. This keeps the sizes of the continents correct in comparison to one another. The shapes of areas near the Equator are accurate, but areas near the Poles, such as Greenland and Antarctica, are stretched.

THE BIGGEST, HIGHEST, AND LONGEST ON EARTH

WHAT IS THE LONGEST river on Earth? How high is Mount Everest? Which is the world's biggest island? You can find the answers to all these questions below. Each of the sections is about one type of geographical feature – mountains, for example. The section contains the highest mountain on Earth – Mt Everest – along with a selection of other mountains from around the world.

THE CONTINENTS

EUROPE
10,498,000 sq km
(4,053,309 sq miles)

ASIA
43,608,800 sq km
(16,838,365 sq miles)

NORTH AMERICA
25,349,000 sq km
(9,785,000 sq miles)

AFRICA
30,335,000 sq km
(11,712,434 sq miles)

ANTARCTICA
14,000,000 sq km
(5,400,000 sq miles)

AUSTRALASIA
8,923,000 sq km
(3,445,197 sq miles)

SOUTH AMERICA
17,835,000 sq km
(6,886,000 sq miles)

THE OCEANS

ATLANTIC OCEAN
82,217,000 sq km
(31,736,000 sq miles)

INDIAN OCEAN
73,481,000 sq km
(28,364,000 sq miles)

PACIFIC OCEAN
165,384,000 sq km
(63,838,000 sq miles)

WATERFALLS

ANGEL	SUTHERLAND	GAVARNIE	JOG	VICTORIA	NIAGARA	FAIRY	VETTISFOSS	RIBBON	GIESSBACH
(Venezuela)	(New Zealand)	(France)	(India)	(Zambia-Zimbabwe)	(United States-Canada)	(United States)	(Norway)	(United States)	(Switzerland)
979 m	580 m	422 m	253 m	108 m	55 m	213 m	274 m	491 m	604 m
(3,212 ft)	(1,904 ft)	(1,385 ft)	(830 ft)	(355 ft)	(182 ft)	(700 ft)	(900 ft)	(1,612 ft)	(1,982 ft)

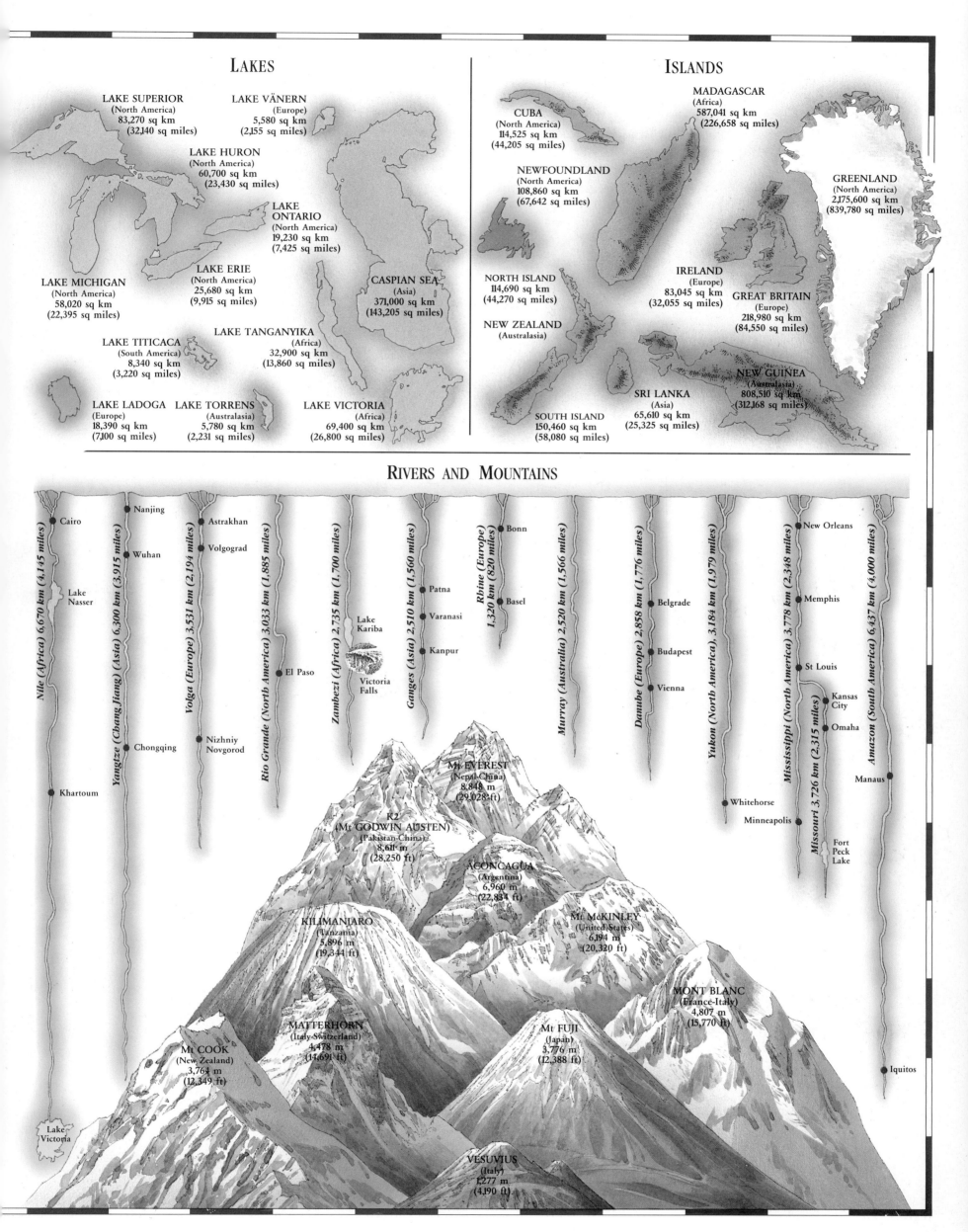

LAKES

LAKE SUPERIOR
(North America)
83,270 sq km
(32,140 sq miles)

LAKE VÄNERN
(Europe)
5,580 sq km
(2,155 sq miles)

LAKE HURON
(North America)
60,700 sq km
(23,430 sq miles)

LAKE ONTARIO
(North America)
19,230 sq km
(7,425 sq miles)

LAKE MICHIGAN
(North America)
58,020 sq km
(22,395 sq miles)

LAKE ERIE
(North America)
25,680 sq km
(9,915 sq miles)

CASPIAN SEA
(Asia)
371,000 sq km
(143,205 sq miles)

LAKE TITICACA
(South America)
8,340 sq km
(3,220 sq miles)

LAKE TANGANYIKA
(Africa)
32,900 sq km
(13,860 sq miles)

LAKE LADOGA
(Europe)
18,390 sq km
(7,100 sq miles)

LAKE TORRENS
(Australasia)
5,780 sq km
(2,231 sq miles)

LAKE VICTORIA
(Africa)
69,400 sq km
(26,800 sq miles)

ISLANDS

CUBA
(North America)
114,525 sq km
(44,205 sq miles)

MADAGASCAR
(Africa)
587,041 sq km
(226,658 sq miles)

NEWFOUNDLAND
(North America)
108,860 sq km
(67,642 sq miles)

GREENLAND
(North America)
2,175,600 sq km
(839,780 sq miles)

NORTH ISLAND
114,690 sq km
(44,270 sq miles)

IRELAND
(Europe)
83,045 sq km
(32,055 sq miles)

NEW ZEALAND
(Australasia)

GREAT BRITAIN
(Europe)
218,980 sq km
(84,550 sq miles)

SRI LANKA
(Asia)
65,610 sq km
(25,325 sq miles)

NEW GUINEA
(Australasia)
808,510 sq km
(312,168 sq miles)

SOUTH ISLAND
150,460 sq km
(58,080 sq miles)

RIVERS AND MOUNTAINS

Nile (Africa) 6,670 km (4,145 miles) — Cairo, Lake Nasser, Khartoum

Yangtze (Chang Jiang) (Asia) 6,300 km (3,915 miles) — Nanjing, Wuhan, Chongqing

Volga (Europe) 3,531 km (2,194 miles) — Astrakhan, Volgograd, Nizhniy Novgorod

Rio Grande (North America) 3,033 km (1,885 miles) — El Paso

Zambezi (Africa) 2,735 km (1,700 miles) — Lake Kariba, Victoria Falls

Ganges (Asia) 2,510 km (1,560 miles) — Patna, Varanasi, Kanpur

Rhine (Europe) 1,320 km (820 miles) — Bonn, Basel

Murray (Australia) 2,520 km (1,566 miles)

Danube (Europe) 2,858 km (1,776 miles) — Belgrade, Budapest, Vienna

Yukon (North America) 3,184 km (1,979 miles) — Whitehorse

Mississippi (North America) 3,778 km (2,348 miles) — New Orleans, Memphis, St Louis, Minneapolis

Missouri 3,726 km (2,315 miles) — Kansas City, Omaha, Fort Peck Lake

Amazon (South America) 6,437 km (4,000 miles) — Manaus, Iquitos

Mt EVEREST
(Nepal-China)
8,848 m
(29,028 ft)

K2
(Mt GODWIN AUSTEN)
(Pakistan-China)
8,611 m
(28,250 ft)

ACONCAGUA
(Argentina)
6,960 m
(22,834 ft)

KILIMANJARO
(Tanzania)
5,896 m
(19,344 ft)

Mt McKINLEY
(United States)
6,194 m
(20,320 ft)

MONT BLANC
(France-Italy)
4,807 m
(15,770 ft)

MATTERHORN
(Italy-Switzerland)
4,478 m
(14,691 ft)

Mt FUJI
(Japan)
3,776 m
(12,388 ft)

Mt COOK
(New Zealand)
3,764 m
(12,349 ft)

Lake Victoria

VESUVIUS
(Italy)
1,277 m
(4,190 ft)

WHERE PEOPLE LIVE

THE TOTAL POPULATION of the world is more than 5.5 billion people. No-one knows the exact figure, as it is constantly rising. The population of the world is growing faster now than ever before. It has doubled since 1950, and many experts believe that it will double again within the next 40 years.

The population of the world is not spread evenly around the globe. Many of the most densely populated countries are in Europe and Asia. In the Netherlands, for example, an average of 360 people live in each square kilometre of land. In contrast, Australia has an average of only two people per square kilometre.

POPULATION BY CONTINENT

The diagrams below show how many people live in each of the continents. Antarctica is the only continent which has no permanent population: the only people who live there are scientists and engineers.

👤 = 10 million people

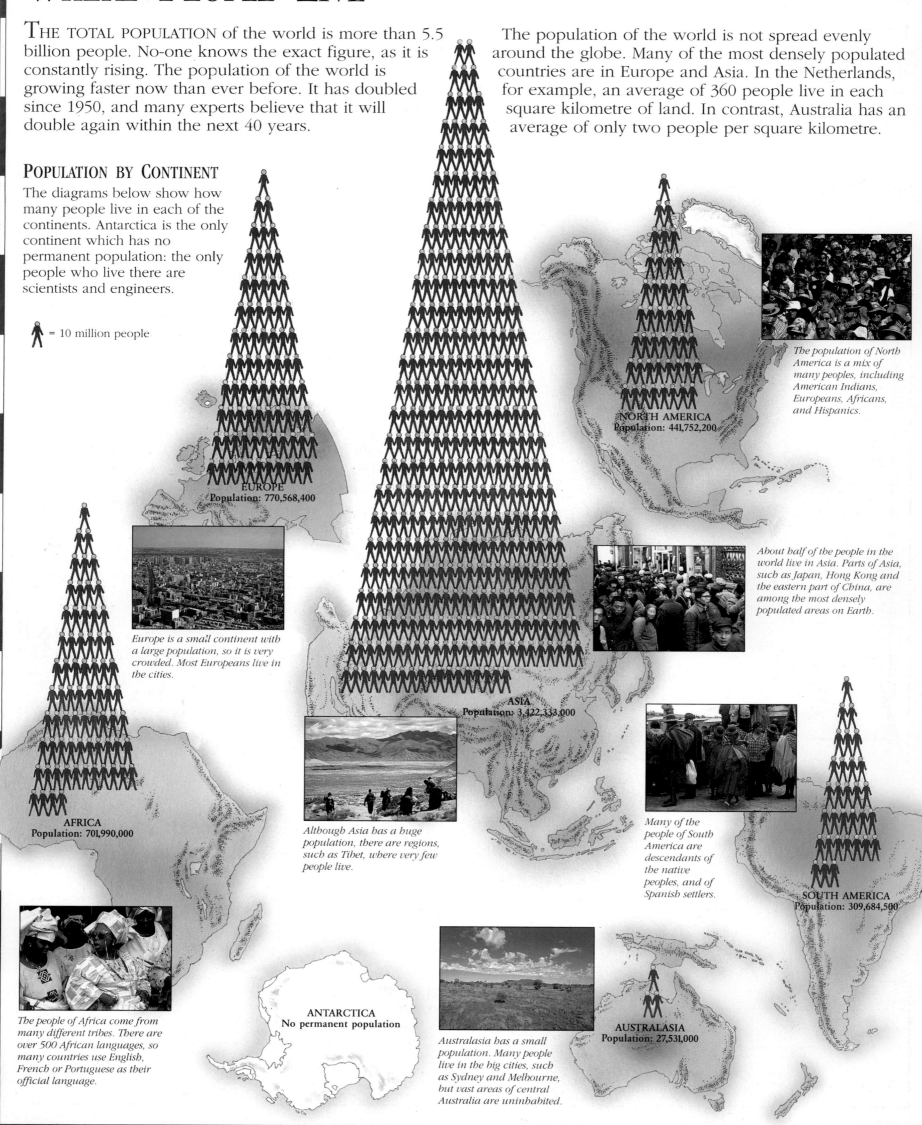

EUROPE
Population: 770,568,400

Europe is a small continent with a large population, so it is very crowded. Most Europeans live in the cities.

NORTH AMERICA
Population: 441,752,200

The population of North America is a mix of many peoples, including American Indians, Europeans, Africans, and Hispanics.

ASIA
Population: 3,422,333,000

About half of the people in the world live in Asia. Parts of Asia, such as Japan, Hong Kong and the eastern part of China, are among the most densely populated areas on Earth.

Although Asia has a huge population, there are regions, such as Tibet, where very few people live.

AFRICA
Population: 701,990,000

The people of Africa come from many different tribes. There are over 500 African languages, so many countries use English, French or Portuguese as their official language.

ANTARCTICA
No permanent population

Australasia has a small population. Many people live in the big cities, such as Sydney and Melbourne, but vast areas of central Australia are uninhabited.

Many of the people of South America are descendants of the native peoples, and of Spanish settlers.

SOUTH AMERICA
Population: 309,684,500

AUSTRALASIA
Population: 27,531,000

HOW TO USE THIS ATLAS

THE MAPS IN THIS ATLAS are split into a number of sections. There is one section for each of the continents: Antarctica, North America, South America, Europe, Asia, Africa, and Australasia. At the start of each section is a map of the whole continent, like the one of North America shown at the bottom of this page. Following this are a series of regional maps, like the one of France below, which show all the countries in that continent. This page shows how to use these maps and explains what the symbols on the maps mean.

NATIONAL FLAGS
The flags of all the countries on the map are shown like this.

BORDERING COUNTRIES
Countries which lie around the edges of the area shown on the map are coloured yellow.

USING THE GRID
The grid around the outside of the page helps you to find places on the map. For example, to find the city of Paris, look its name up in the index on pages 77–80. Next to the word Paris are the reference numbers 39 E13. The first number shows that Paris is on page 39 of the atlas. The second number means that it is in square E13 of the grid. Turn to page 39. Trace across from the letter E on the grid and then down from the number 13. Paris is situated in the area where the two meet.

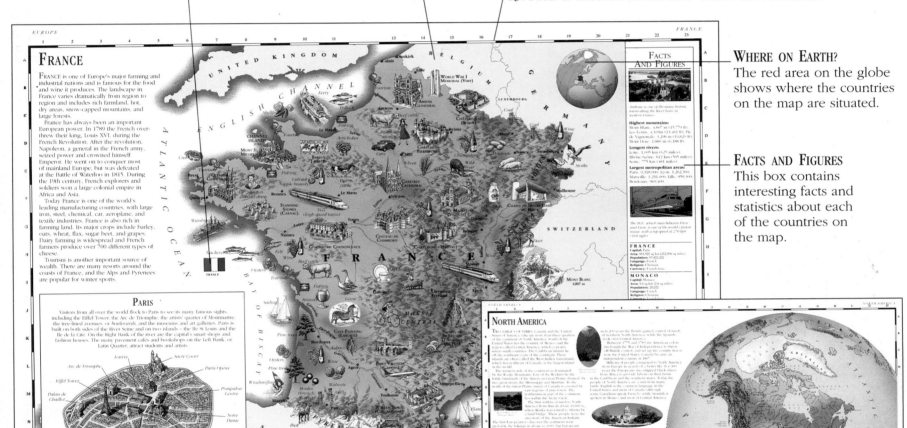

WHERE ON EARTH?
The red area on the globe shows where the countries on the map are situated.

FACTS AND FIGURES
This box contains interesting facts and statistics about each of the countries on the map.

SPECIAL FEATURES
Features like this one give further information about a place or feature of interest on the map.

SCALE
You can use the scale to see how big the countries are, and how far it is from one place to another. Not all the maps have been drawn to the same scale.

POLITICAL MAP
This shows all the countries in the continent.

GEOGRAPHICAL MAP
This map of the continent shows all the main geographical features, such as rivers, mountains, lakes and deserts.

KEY TO THE MAPS

Capital City	City	Country name	Range of mountains	An individual mountain with its height	River	Lake	A specific building or place	A product, animal, plant or activity, that is found all over the region
● LONDON	● Bristol	FRANCE	△ ALPS	△ MT EVEREST 8,848 m	Ganges	LAKE TITICACA	THE LEANING TOWER OF PISA	Wine

THE ARCTIC

THE ARCTIC CIRCLE contains the northernmost parts of North America, Europe and Asia, along with most of the island of Greenland. The temperature in the Arctic is so low that much of the Arctic Ocean is permanently frozen. Within the Arctic Circle, there are days in midwinter when the Sun never rises, and days in midsummer when it never sets. Despite the harsh climate, a wide variety of animals and plants live in the Arctic. The main human inhabitants are the Inuit (Eskimos) and the Sami (Lapps).

The island of Greenland is anything but green – much of it is permanently covered by ice. The Inuit have lived in Greenland since about 2500 BC. The first Europeans to settle there were the Vikings, in about AD 986. Today Greenland is a self-governing province of Denmark.

FACTS AND FIGURES

Flowing river of ice, called a glacier, in Greenland.

Highest mountain:
Mt Gunnbjorn (Greenland), 3,700 m (12,139 ft.

Beneath the North Pole:
There is no solid land. This was proved in 1958 when a submarine, the USS Nautilus, travelled under the ice.

Flight Paths over the Arctic:
These provide the shortest air connections between Europe and North America.

GREENLAND
Area: 2,175,600 sq km (839,780 sq miles)
Population: 56,000

ARCTIC CIRCLE (approx. 66.5° North)

ALASKA

Kittiwake

Ptarmigan

Elk

Moose

Evenk (Eskimo)

CHUKCHI SEA

Chukchi (Eskimo)

NORTHERN LIMIT OF FOREST

Snowy owl

Gray whale

Large seal

Reindeer

Polar bear

Arctic tern

Caribou

Glaucous gull

Lemmings

Arctic fox

Polar bear

White whale

Ermine

Long-tailed skua

SIBERIAN RUSSIAN FEDERATION

Snow geese

Musk oxen

Arctic tern

ARCTIC OCEAN

Robert Peary (USA) claimed he was the first person to reach the North Pole in 1909.

SEVERNAYA ZEMLYA

Skua

Eskimo with reindeer

○ NORTH POLE

Arctic tern

Arctic wolves

Brent goose

Polar bear

Arctic hares

Arctic fox

Inuit (Eskimo)

Long-tailed skua

Barnacle goose

Bearded seal

Snow goose

Inuit (Eskimo)

Guillemots

NOVAYA ZEMLYA

Walruses

BAFFIN BAY

Ptarmigan

Lemmings

Ringed seal

Polar bear

Walrus

Nenet (Eskimo)

Narwhals

Coal

SVALBARD ISLANDS

Right whale

Walrus

Elk

Fishing trawler

Walrus

Musk oxen

Killer whale

BARENTS SEA

Great black-backed gulls

Guillemots

Godthåb

GREENLAND (DENMARK)

Barnacle goose

Hooded seal

Grey seals

MT GUNNBJØRN 3,700 m

MT FOREL △ 3,360 m

Harp seals

Cod

Lapp with reindeer

Humpback whale

Ringed seal

Puffins

ICELAND

Sperm whale

LAPLAND

LIMIT OF PERMANENT PACK ICE

| 0 | 200 | 400 | 600 | 800 Kilometres |
| 0 | 125 | 250 | 375 | 500 Miles |

THE ANTARCTIC

THE ANTARCTIC has the coldest and harshest climate in the world. Nearly all the land is covered by ice, on average about 2,000 m (6,562 ft) thick. The size of the ice sheet varies between the seasons. In summer the ice at the edge of the sheet melts or breaks off to form icebergs. In winter the sea at the edge of the ice sheet freezes again and is called pack ice. There are very few plants. The animals that live in the Antarctic, such as seals and penguins, depend on the sea for their supply of food.

Although no country owns Antarctica, a number of countries claim territory, and many have bases there for scientific research. Even the small population of scientists dwindles during the bitter Antarctic winter, when blizzards last for days. The world's coldest temperature of -89.2°C (-128.6°F) was recorded at Vostok Station in July 1983.

FACTS AND FIGURES

The sea around the Antarctic is covered by drifting pack ice for most of the year.

Antarctica contains 90 per cent of all the world's ice: If it melted, the level of the seas throughout the world would rise by 60 m (200 ft) and drown all the coastal towns and cities.

CONTINENT OF ANTARCTICA
Area: 14,000,000 sq km (5,400,000 sq miles)
Inhabitants: Scientists and engineers only
Climate: Cold, dry and windy

Imperial shags

Gentoo penguins

Antarctic cod

Chinstrap penguin

Elephant seals

Iceberg

Antarctic petrels

Crabeater seal

Giant petrel

Survey ship

HALLEY STATION (UK)

Emperor penguins

Adélie penguins

Fish factory ship

Antarctic fulmars

Humpback whale

Leopard seal

Emperor penguins

South polar skua

MOLODEZHNAYA STATION (Russia)

ANTARCTIC CIRCLE (approx. 66.5° South)

SOUTH ATLANTIC OCEAN

WEDDELL SEA

Right whale

Crabeater seal

Piked whale

Crabeater seals

Elephant seals

Snow petrels

Emperor penguins

RONNE ICE SHELF

Survey plane

QUEEN MAUD LAND

Weddell seal

Toothfish

Krill

Crabeater seal

Antarctic fulmar

Ross seal

MARIE BYRD LAND

AMUNDSEN SEA

BELLINGSHAUSEN SEA

AMUNDSEN-SCOTT STATION (USA)

ANTARCTICA

○ SOUTH POLE

Emperor penguins

Antarctic petrels

Roald Amundsen (Norway) first reached South Pole December 1911.

Robert Scott (UK) reached South Pole January 1912.

Adélie penguins

Elephant seals

Snow petrels

Blue whale

South polar skua

Iceberg

Tourist liner

ROSS ICE SHELF

VOSTOK STATION (Russia)

McMURDO AIR STATION (USA)

Leopard seal

Snow petrels

Emperor penguins

WILKES LAND

Adélie penguins

Krill

CASEY BASE (Australia)

Antarctic cod

SOUTH PACIFIC OCEAN

Fin whale

Ross seal

Adélie penguins

Chinstrap penguins

DUMONT D'URVILLE STATION (France)

LIMIT OF PERMANENT PACK ICE

Killer whale

Leopard seal

Ice fish

INDIAN OCEAN

NORTH AMERICA

TWO LARGE COUNTRIES, Canada and the United States of America, take up more than three-quarters of the continent of North America. South of the United States lies the country of Mexico and the region called Central America, which contains seven small countries. The Caribbean islands lie off the southeast coast of the continent. These islands are often called the West Indies. Greenland, which lies northeast of Canada, is the largest island in the world.

The western side of the continent is dominated by the Rocky Mountains. East of the Rockies lie the fertile farmlands of the American Great Plains, drained by two great rivers, the Mississippi and Missouri. To the north of the Great Plains, much of Canada is covered by vast regions of pine forest. The northernmost part of the continent lies within the Arctic Circle.

The first settlers crossed to North America from Asia in about 40,000 BC, when Alaska was joined to Siberia by a land bridge. These people were the ancestors of the American Indians. The first Europeans to discover the continent were probably the Vikings in about AD 1000, but Europeans only began to settle there in the 16th century. Over the

Mountain scenery, Alberta, Canada.

Ancient Maya city of Palenque, Mexico.

next 200 years the British gained control of much of northern North America, while the Spanish took over Central America.

Between 1775 and 1783 the American colonists fought the War of Independence to throw off British control, and set up the country that is now the United States. Canada became an independent country in 1867.

Millions of people emigrated to North America from Europe in search of a better life. For 300 years the Europeans also shipped black slaves from Africa to provide labour on their farms in the Caribbean and the southern states. Today the people of North America are a mix from many lands. English is the common language in the United States and most of Canada (although some Canadians speak French), while Spanish is spoken in Mexico and most of Central America.

The Capitol Building, Washington DC, United States.

FACTS ABOUT NORTH AMERICA

Area: 25,349,000 sq km (9,785,000 sq miles).

Population: 441,752,200.

Number of independent countries: 23.

Largest countries: Canada, 9,976,139 sq km (3,851,817 sq miles); United States, 9,372,614 sq km (3,618,794 sq miles); Mexico, 1,967,183 sq km (761,530 sq miles).

Most populated countries: United States, 257,800,000; Mexico, 90,000,000.

Largest metropolitan areas: Mexico City (Mexico), 15,047,700; Los Angeles (United States), 8,863,200; New York City (United States), 8,546,800; Chicago (United States) 8,065,600.

Longest rivers: Mississippi-Missouri, 6,019 km (3,740 miles); Mackenzie, 4,240 km (2,635 miles); Yukon, 3,184 km (1,979 miles).

Highest mountains: Mt McKinley (United States), 6,194 m (20,320 ft); Mt Logan (Canada), 5,951 m (19,524 ft).

Largest lakes: Lake Superior (United States-Canada), 83,270 sq km (32,140 sq miles); Lake Huron (United States-Canada), 60,700 sq km (23,430 sq miles); Great Bear Lake (Canada), 31,790 sq km (12,270 sq miles).

Largest islands: Greenland, 2,175,600 sq km (839,780 sq miles); Baffin Island, 476,070 sq km (183,760 sq miles).

Hottest place: Death Valley in California (United States) is the hottest place in North America. In 1917 the temperature there reached 48.9°C (120°F).

World's shortest river: The Roe River, which flows into the Missouri near Great Falls in Montana (United States), is only 61m (200 ft) long.

World's highest geyser: Steamboat Geyser in Yellowstone National Park (United States) can reach 115 m (380 ft).

World's longest frontier: The border between Canada and the United States measures 6,416 km (3,987 miles).

ARCTIC OCEAN

GREENLAND (DENMARK)

ALASKA (USA)

CANADA

PACIFIC OCEAN

ATLANTIC OCEAN

USA

MEXICO

BAHAMAS

CUBA
HAITI
DOMINICAN REPUBLIC
PUERTO RICO (USA)
JAMAICA

BELIZE
GUATEMALA
HONDURAS
EL SALVADOR
NICARAGUA
COSTA RICA
PANAMA

KEY
1 ST CHRISTOPHER & NEVIS
2 ANTIGUA & BARBUDA
3 GUADELOUPE (France)
4 DOMINICA
5 MARTINIQUE (France)
6 ST LUCIA
7 ST VINCENT
8 BARBADOS
9 GRENADA
10 TRINIDAD & TOBAGO

ALEUTIAN ISLANDS

HAWAIIAN ISLANDS

P

13 14 15 16 17 18 19 20 21 22 23

A
B
C
D

A S I A

E U R O P E

A R C T I C   O C E A N

G R E E N L A N D

ELLESMERE ISLAND

BAFFIN BAY

BANKS ISLAND

DAVIS STRAIT

BEAUFORT SEA

VICTORIA ISLAND

BAFFIN ISLAND

BERING STRAIT

BROOKS RANGE

Yukon

LABRADOR SEA

GREAT BEAR LAKE

▲ Mt McKINLEY 6,194 m

MACKENZIE MTS

Mackenzie

KODIAK ISLAND

GULF OF ALASKA

▲ Mt LOGAN 5,951 m

GREAT SLAVE LAKE

HUDSON BAY

NEWFOUNDLAND

LAKE ATHABASCA

QUEEN CHARLOTTE ISLANDS

LAKE WINNIPEG

Fraser

VANCOUVER ISLAND

LAKE MANITOBA

R O C K Y   M T S

G R E A T   P L A I N S

LAKE SUPERIOR

LAKE HURON

St Lawrence

LAKE ONTARIO

CAPE COD

LAKE MICHIGAN

LAKE ERIE

Missouri

A P P A L A C H I A N M T S

P A C I F I C

G R E A T   B A S I N

GREAT SALT LAKE

Colorado

Mississippi

Rio Grande

GULF OF CALIFORNIA

GULF OF MEXICO

LESSER ANTILLES

GREATER ANTILLES

YUCATAN PENINSULA

GULF OF HONDURAS

CARIBBEAN SEA

▲ CITLALTÉPETL 5,700 m

LAKE NICARAGUA

S O U T H   A M E R I C A

O C E A N

A T L A N T I C   O C E A N

L
M
N
O

13 14 15 16 17 18 19 20 21 22 23

CANADA AND ALASKA

CANADA is the world's second largest country, yet its population is small – only about one-tenth that of the smaller United States, its southern neighbour. More than half of all Canadians live in the area around the Great Lakes and the St Lawrence River. In the centre of Canada lie the Prairies, a flat plain used mainly for grazing cattle and growing wheat. Northern Canada is covered by vast areas of forest and tundra, while the west of the country is dominated by the Rocky Mountains.

The first inhabitants of Canada were the Indian and Inuit (Eskimo) peoples. French and British settlers started to move

there in the 17th century. Although Canada became part of the British Empire, the French influence has always been strong and many Canadians still speak French today. Canada became an independent country in 1867.

Alaska, which lies to the northwest of Canada, is the largest state in the United States. Alaska is one of the world's major oil-producing regions.

ARCTIC OCEAN

QUEEN ELIZABETH ISLANDS

BEAUFORT SEA

BERING STRAIT

Polar bear

Ice-breaker ship

BANKS ISLAND

Snow geese

VICTORIA ISLAND

Caribou

Oil

Oil

BERING SEA

Dog-drawn sledge

Musk ox

Oil

UNITED STATES

Salmon

Spruce

ALASKA (USA)

Yukon

Fairbanks

Furs

GREAT BEAR LAKE

Wolves

Fur seal

Walruses

Mr McKINLEY 6,194 m

Dall sheep

Anchorage

Zinc and lead

MACKENZIE MTS

Mackenzie

Silver

NORTHWEST TERR

Mr LOGAN 5,951 m

YUKON TERRITORY

Whitehorse

Yellowknife

Paper birch

Moose

GREAT SLAVE LAKE

Right whale

Oil tanker

ROCKY MTS

COAST MTS

Juneau

Douglas fir

Skiing

Peace

LAKE ATHABASCA

A

MONTREAL

Montreal, situated in the province of Quebec, is one of Canada's largest cities. Two-thirds of the people in Montreal speak French, making it the second largest French-speaking city in the world after Paris. French traders founded the city, which they called Ville-Marie, in 1642. It was built on Montreal Island in the St Lawrence river. Today, Montreal is Canada's leading port and a major trading and manufacturing centre.

BRITISH COLUMBIA

Grizzly bear

Salmon

ALBERTA

Mountie

Oil

SASKATCHEWAN

QUEEN CHARLOTTE ISLANDS

Indian totem pole

Calgary skyline

Edmonton

Halibut

PACIFIC OCEAN

Fraser

Calgary

VANCOUVER ISLAND

Vancouver

Wheat

Regi

Victoria

The Calgary Stampede (annual rodeo)

U

0   200   400   600

0 100 200 300 400

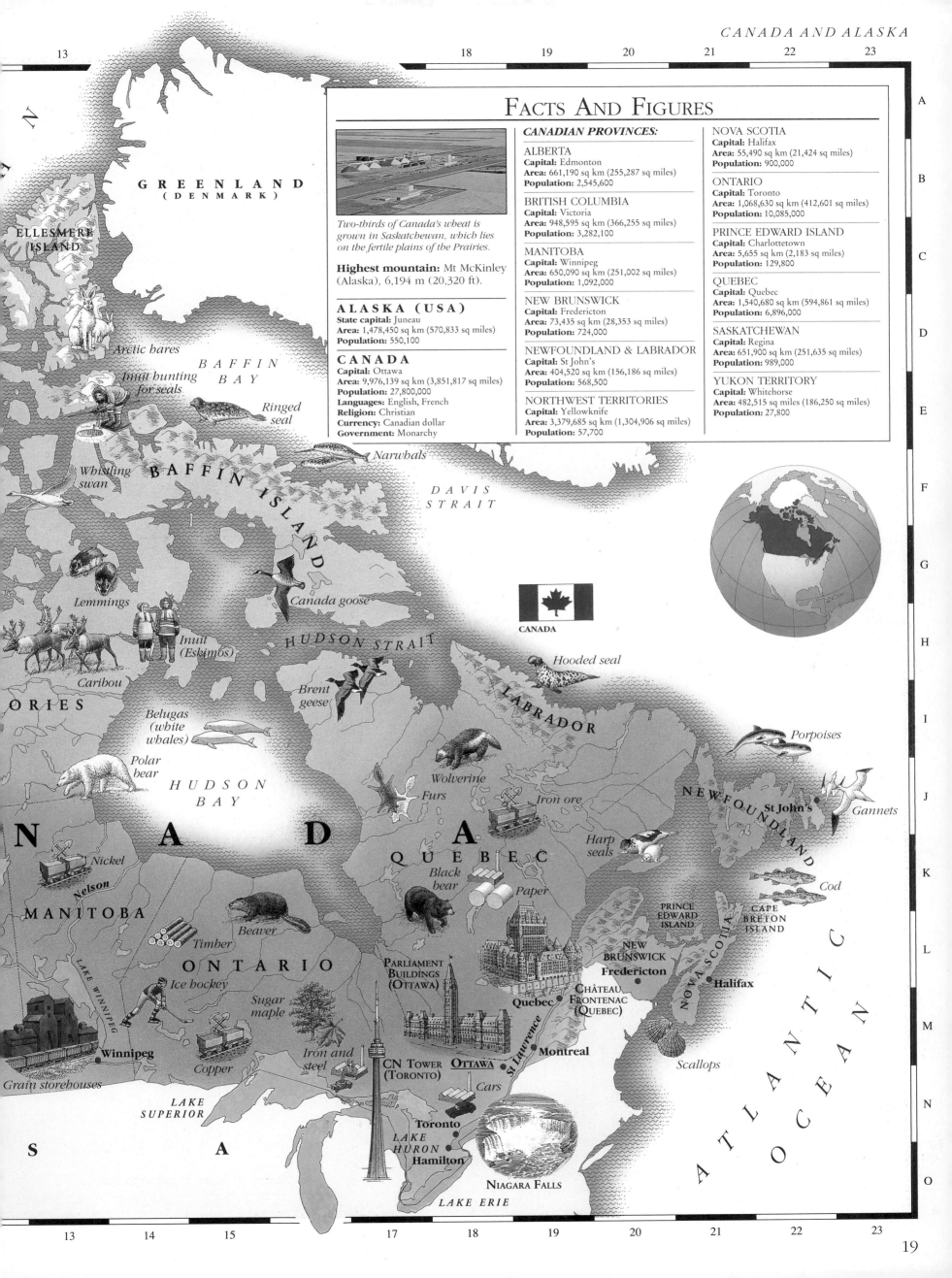

13 18 19 20 21 22 23

GREENLAND
(DENMARK)

ELLESMERE
ISLAND

Arctic hares

Inuit hunting for seals

BAFFIN
BAY

Ringed seal

FACTS AND FIGURES

Two-thirds of Canada's wheat is grown in Saskatchewan, which lies on the fertile plains of the Prairies.

Highest mountain: Mt McKinley (Alaska), 6,194 m (20,320 ft).

ALASKA (USA)
State capital: Juneau
Area: 1,478,450 sq km (570,833 sq miles)
Population: 550,100

CANADA
Capital: Ottawa
Area: 9,976,139 sq km (3,851,817 sq miles)
Population: 27,800,000
Languages: English, French
Religion: Christian
Currency: Canadian dollar
Government: Monarchy

CANADIAN PROVINCES:

ALBERTA
Capital: Edmonton
Area: 661,190 sq km (255,287 sq miles)
Population: 2,545,600

BRITISH COLUMBIA
Capital: Victoria
Area: 948,595 sq km (366,255 sq miles)
Population: 3,282,100

MANITOBA
Capital: Winnipeg
Area: 650,090 sq km (251,002 sq miles)
Population: 1,092,000

NEW BRUNSWICK
Capital: Fredericton
Area: 73,435 sq km (28,353 sq miles)
Population: 724,000

NEWFOUNDLAND & LABRADOR
Capital: St John's
Area: 404,520 sq km (156,186 sq miles)
Population: 568,500

NORTHWEST TERRITORIES
Capital: Yellowknife
Area: 3,379,685 sq km (1,304,906 sq miles)
Population: 57,700

NOVA SCOTIA
Capital: Halifax
Area: 55,490 sq km (21,424 sq miles)
Population: 900,000

ONTARIO
Capital: Toronto
Area: 1,068,630 sq km (412,601 sq miles)
Population: 10,085,000

PRINCE EDWARD ISLAND
Capital: Charlottetown
Area: 5,655 sq km (2,183 sq miles)
Population: 129,800

QUEBEC
Capital: Quebec
Area: 1,540,680 sq km (594,861 sq miles)
Population: 6,896,000

SASKATCHEWAN
Capital: Regina
Area: 651,900 sq km (251,635 sq miles)
Population: 989,000

YUKON TERRITORY
Capital: Whitehorse
Area: 482,515 sq miles (186,250 sq miles)
Population: 27,800

Narwhals

Whistling swan

BAFFIN ISLAND

DAVIS STRAIT

Lemmings

Canada goose

Inuit (Eskimos)

HUDSON STRAIT

CANADA

Caribou

Brent geese

LABRADOR

Hooded seal

ORIES

Belugas (white whales)

Polar bear

HUDSON BAY

Wolverine

Furs

Iron ore

Porpoises

NEWFOUNDLAND

St John's

Gannets

N   A   D   A

QUEBEC

Harp seals

Cod

Nickel

Black bear

Paper

PRINCE EDWARD ISLAND

CAPE BRETON ISLAND

Nelson

MANITOBA

Beaver

NOVA SCOTIA

NEW BRUNSWICK

Fredericton

Halifax

Timber

ONTARIO

Ice hockey

Sugar maple

Parliament Buildings (OTTAWA)

Château Frontenac (QUEBEC)

Quebec

LAKE WINNIPEG

Winnipeg

Iron and steel

Copper

CN TOWER (TORONTO)

OTTAWA

Cars

St. Lawrence

Montreal

Scallops

Grain storehouses

LAKE SUPERIOR

Toronto

LAKE HURON

Hamilton

Niagara Falls

LAKE ERIE

S   A

ATLANTIC OCEAN

THE UNITED STATES

THE UNITED STATES OF AMERICA is one of the largest and richest countries in the world. It is made up of 50 states, each of which has its own government. The national government is based in the capital, Washington DC. The letters "DC" stand for District of Columbia, the name of the area in which the city is situated.

The country is dominated by two mountain ranges – the Rockies in the west and the Appalachians in the east. In between lie the flat, fertile Great Plains, which are used for farming. The United States is rich in natural resources. It has large deposits of raw materials, such as iron, coal, and oil, which are needed to produce industrial goods. These resources have helped the country to become the world's greatest industrial manufacturer. The United States is also rich in farmland, and exports large amounts of agricultural produce, especially cereals, cotton, and tobacco. Most years, the United States exports more grain than all the other countries of the world combined.

The United States is often described as a "melting pot" because its population is a mix of many peoples. The country's first inhabitants were the American Indians. Later, settlers came from all over Europe, especially the UK, Italy, Ireland, and Poland. The United States' black population are the descendants of slaves who were brought to America from Africa. More recent arrivals include Hispanics (Spanish-speakers) from Mexico and South America, and Asians.

THE NORTHEASTERN STATES

THE NORTHEASTERN part of the United States is the most crowded region in the country. Large numbers of people live near the Atlantic coast in the great cities of Boston, New York, Philadelphia, Baltimore, and Washington. This coast was the first area of the United States to be settled by Europeans. In 1620 colonists from England, who are known as the "Pilgrim Fathers", established the first settlement at New Plymouth, Massachusetts, in the region that is still called New England.

Farther inland lie the Great Lakes, the largest group of freshwater lakes in the world, which form part of the border between the United States and Canada. The region around the Great Lakes has the greatest concentration of industry in the United States. The biggest cities are Chicago, Pittsburgh, and Detroit, which is known as the "Motor City" because it is the centre of the American car industry. The main products of the area are iron and steel, machinery, cars, chemicals, coal, and textiles.

West and southwest of the Great Lakes are the states of Minnesota, Wisconsin, and Iowa, which lie on the flat land of the Great Plains. Much of the United States' wheat and maize is grown in this area, which is often called the "farm belt".

FACTS AND FIGURES

The area of New England is famous for its spectacular forests and old wooden houses.

THE UNITED STATES
Capital: Washington DC
Area: 9,372,614 sq km (3,618,794 sq miles)
Population: 257,800,000
Language: English
Religion: Christian
Currency: US dollar
Government: Republic

UNITED STATES

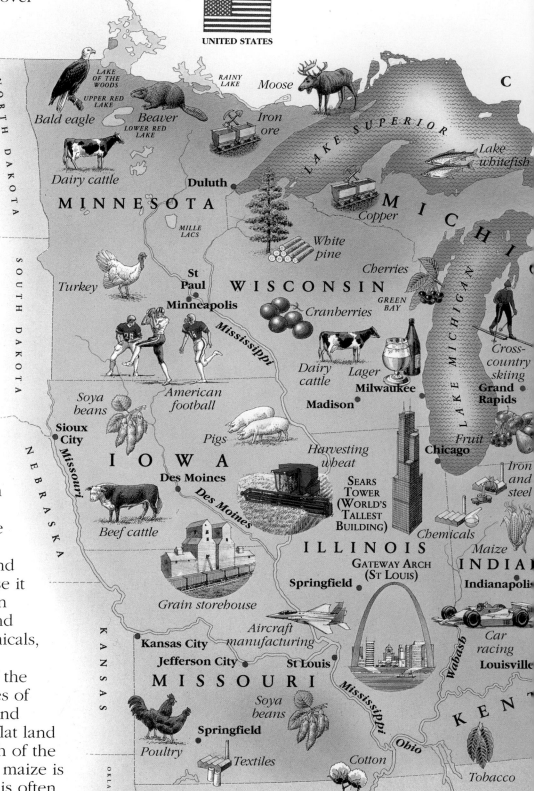

13 14 15 16 17 18 19 20 21 22 23

NEW YORK CITY

The skyline of Manhattan Island in the centre of New York is perhaps the best-known view of any city in the world. It was the first sight of America for the millions of people who emigrated there from Europe during the 19th and early 20th centuries. Today, New York is the largest city in the United States, the country's leading port, and a world financial centre.

FACTS AND FIGURES

The skyline of Chicago is dominated by the Sears Tower – the world's tallest building.

THE NORTHEASTERN STATES:

CONNECTICUT
Capital: Hartford
Area: 12,620 sq km (4,872 sq miles)
Population: 3,287,120

DELAWARE
Capital: Dover
Area: 5,005 sq km (1,932 sq miles)
Population: 666,170

DISTRICT OF COLUMBIA
Area: 163 sq km (63 sq miles)
Population: 606,900

ILLINOIS
Capital: Springfield
Area: 144,120 sq km (55,645 sq miles)
Population: 11,430,600

INDIANA
Capital: Indianapolis
Area: 93,065 sq km (35,932 sq miles)
Population: 5,544,200

IOWA
Capital: Des Moines
Area: 144,950 sq km (55,965 sq miles)
Population: 2,776,800

KENTUCKY
Capital: Frankfort
Area: 102,740 sq km (39,668 sq miles)
Population: 3,685,300

MAINE
Capital: Augusta
Area: 80,275 sq km (30,994 sq miles)
Population: 1,227,900

MARYLAND
Capital: Annapolis
Area: 25,480 sq km (9,837 sq miles)
Population: 4,781,500

MASSACHUSETTS
Capital: Boston
Area: 20,265 sq km (7,824 sq miles)
Population: 6,016,400

MICHIGAN
Capital: Lansing
Area: 147,520 sq km (56,957 sq miles)
Population: 9,295,300

MINNESOTA
Capital: St Paul
Area: 206,030 sq km (79,548 sq miles)
Population: 4,375,100

MISSOURI
Capital: Jefferson City
Area: 178,565 sq km (68,944 sq miles)
Population: 5,117,100

NEW HAMPSHIRE
Capital: Concord
Area: 23,290 sq km (8,992 sq miles)
Population: 1,109,300

NEW JERSEY
Capital: Trenton
Area: 19,340 sq km (7,467 sq miles)
Population: 7,730,200

NEW YORK
Capital: Albany
Area: 122,705 sq km (47,376 sq miles)
Population: 17,990,500

OHIO
Capital: Columbus
Area: 106,200 sq km (41,004 sq miles)
Population: 10,847,100

PENNSYLVANIA
Capital: Harrisburg
Area: 116,260 sq km (44,888 sq miles)
Population: 11,881,600

RHODE ISLAND
Capital: Providence
Area: 2,730 sq km (1,054 sq miles)
Population: 1,003,500

VERMONT
Capital: Montpelier
Area: 24,900 sq km (9,613 sq miles)
Population: 562,800

VIRGINIA
Capital: Richmond
Area: 102,835 sq km (39,695 sq miles)
Population: 6,187,400

WEST VIRGINIA
Capital: Charleston
Area: 62,470 sq km (24,119 sq miles)
Population: 1,793,500

WISCONSIN
Capital: Madison
Area: 140,965 sq km (54,427 sq miles)
Population: 4,891,800

THE SOUTHERN STATES

THE SOUTHERN STATES extend from the Atlantic coast in the east to the Mexican border in the west. Flowing southwards through the region is the Mississippi River, which reaches the Gulf of Mexico at New Orleans. Before the railways were built, the Mississippi was North America's most important trading route.

In the 18th and 19th centuries, the wealth of the South was based on farming. Cotton, tobacco, and other crops were grown on large farms called plantations. The workers on the plantations were black slaves, who were brought over from Africa. In the 1860s a civil war was fought in America between the southern states (the Confederacy) and the northern states (the Union). One of the main causes of the war was that the South refused to get rid of slavery. In 1865, the Union was victorious and the slaves were freed.

In the west of this region lies the huge state of Texas, which is famous for its cattle ranches and its oil. The long peninsula of Florida, in the south-east, is popular for holidays and attracts tourists from all over the world because of its good climate and beautiful beaches.

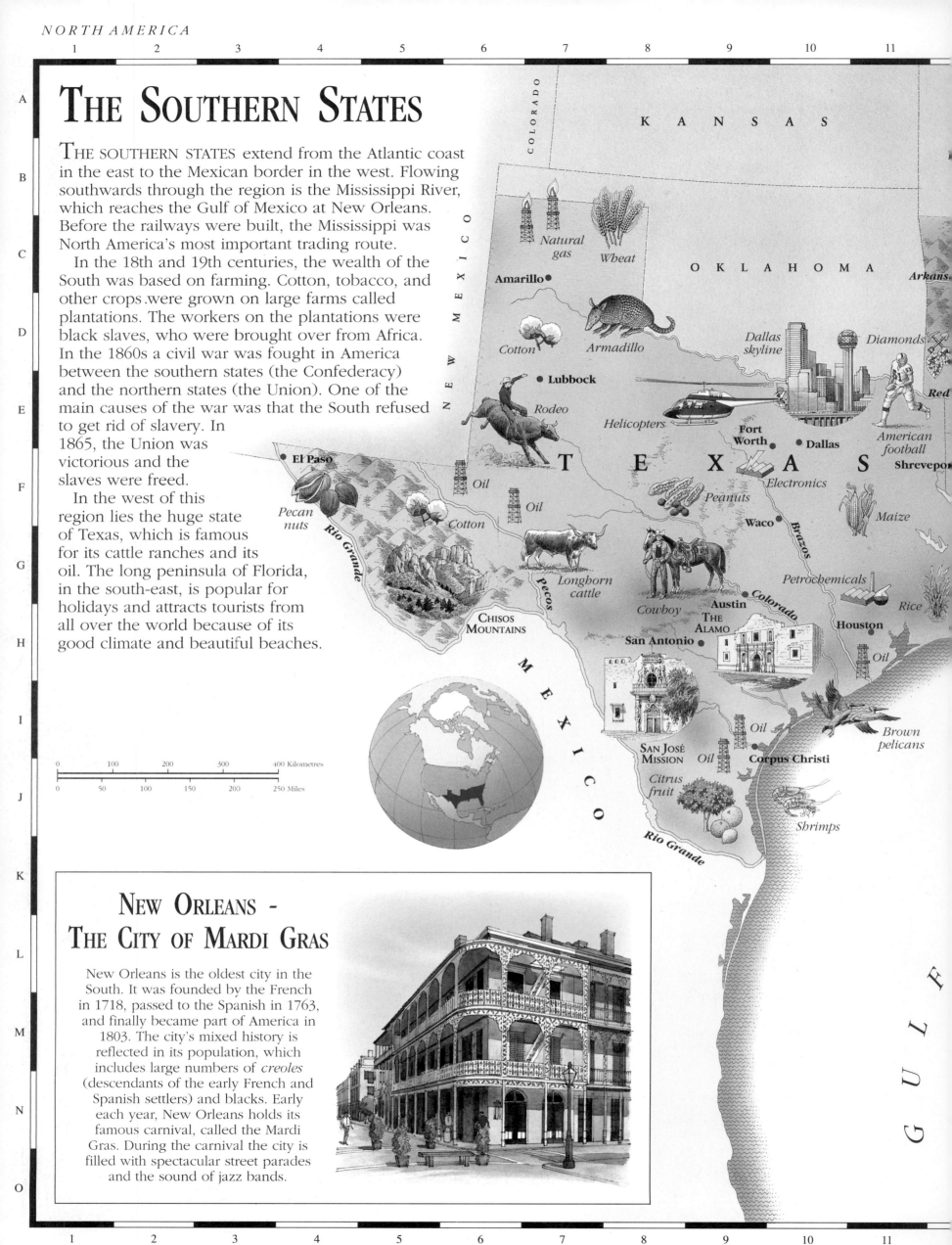

NEW ORLEANS - THE CITY OF MARDI GRAS

New Orleans is the oldest city in the South. It was founded by the French in 1718, passed to the Spanish in 1763, and finally became part of America in 1803. The city's mixed history is reflected in its population, which includes large numbers of *creoles* (descendants of the early French and Spanish settlers) and blacks. Early each year, New Orleans holds its famous carnival, called the Mardi Gras. During the carnival the city is filled with spectacular street parades and the sound of jazz bands.

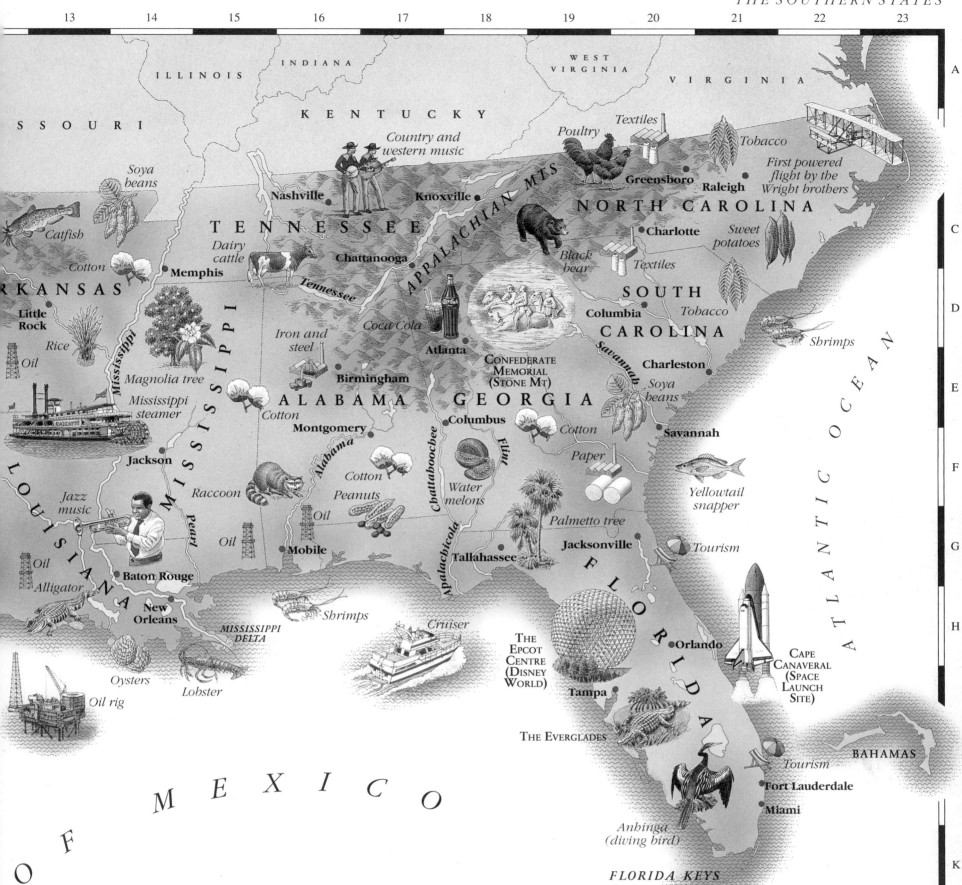

13 14 15 16 17 18 19 20 21 22 23

ILLINOIS
INDIANA
WEST VIRGINIA
VIRGINIA
SSOURI
KENTUCKY
Soya beans
Catfish
Country and western music
Poultry
Textiles
Tobacco
First powered flight by the Wright brothers
Nashville
Knoxville
Greensboro
Raleigh
Cotton
TENNESSEE
NORTH CAROLINA
Memphis
Dairy cattle
Chattanooga
APPALACHIAN MTS
Black bear
Charlotte
Sweet potatoes
Tennessee
ARKANSAS
Iron and steel
Coca Cola
SOUTH
Little Rock
Rice
Atlanta
CONFEDERATE MEMORIAL (STONE MT)
Columbia
Tobacco
CAROLINA
Oil
Magnolia tree
Birmingham
Charleston
Shrimps
MISSISSIPPI
Mississippi steamer
ALABAMA
GEORGIA
Savannah
Soya beans
Mississippi
Cotton
Montgomery
Columbus
Cotton
Savannah
Jackson
Alabama
Cotton
Paper
Jazz music
Raccoon
Peanuts
Water melons
Flint
Yellowtail snapper
LOUISIANA
Oil
Oil
Chattahoochee
Palmetto tree
Oil
Mobile
Jacksonville
Tourism
Baton Rouge
Tallahassee
Apalachicola
FLORIDA
Alligator
New Orleans
Shrimps
Cruiser
THE EPCOT CENTRE (DISNEY WORLD)
Orlando
CAPE CANAVERAL (SPACE LAUNCH SITE)
MISSISSIPPI DELTA
Tampa
Oysters
Lobster
THE EVERGLADES
Oil rig
ATLANTIC OCEAN
Tourism
BAHAMAS
Fort Lauderdale
Miami
Anhinga (diving bird)
GULF OF MEXICO
FLORIDA KEYS

A B C D E F G H K L M N O

FACTS AND FIGURES

The city of Miami in Florida is a popular tourist resort. High-rise hotels line the beach.

Largest metropolitan areas:
Dallas-Fort Worth (Texas), 4,037,300; Houston (Texas), 3,302,000; Atlanta (Georgia), 2,833,600; Miami (Florida), 1,937,100; New Orleans (Louisiana), 1,238,900.

Longest river: Mississippi,

3,778 km (2,348 miles).
World's largest theme park
Disney World, in Florida, covers an area of 113 sq km (44 sq miles). Millions of people visit the park each year.

THE SOUTHERN STATES:

ALABAMA
Capital: Montgomery
Area: 131,485 sq km (50,766 sq miles)
Population: 4,040,600

ARKANSAS
Capital: Little Rock
Area: 134,880 sq km (52,077 sq miles)
Population: 2,350,800

FLORIDA
Capital: Tallahassee
Area: 140,255 sq km (54,152 sq miles)
Population: 12,938,000

GEORGIA
Capital: Atlanta
Area: 150,365 sq km (58,056 sq miles)
Population: 6,478,300

LOUISIANA
Capital: Baton Rouge
Area: 115,310 sq km (44,521 sq miles)
Population: 4,220,000

MISSISSIPPI
Capital: Jackson
Area: 122,335 sq km (47,233 sq miles)
Population: 2,573,300

NORTH CAROLINA
Capital: Raleigh
Area: 126,505 sq km (48,843 sq miles)
Population: 6,628,700

SOUTH CAROLINA
Capital: Columbia
Area: 78,225 sq km (30,202 sq miles)
Population: 3,486,700

TENNESSEE
Capital: Nashville
Area: 106,590 sq km (41,154 sq miles)
Population: 4,877,200

TEXAS
Capital: Austin
Area: 678,620 sq km (262,017 sq miles)
Population: 16,986,500

The state of Texas is famous for its huge cattle ranches, where cowboys still round up the animals on horseback.

13 14 15 16 17 18 19 20 21 22 23

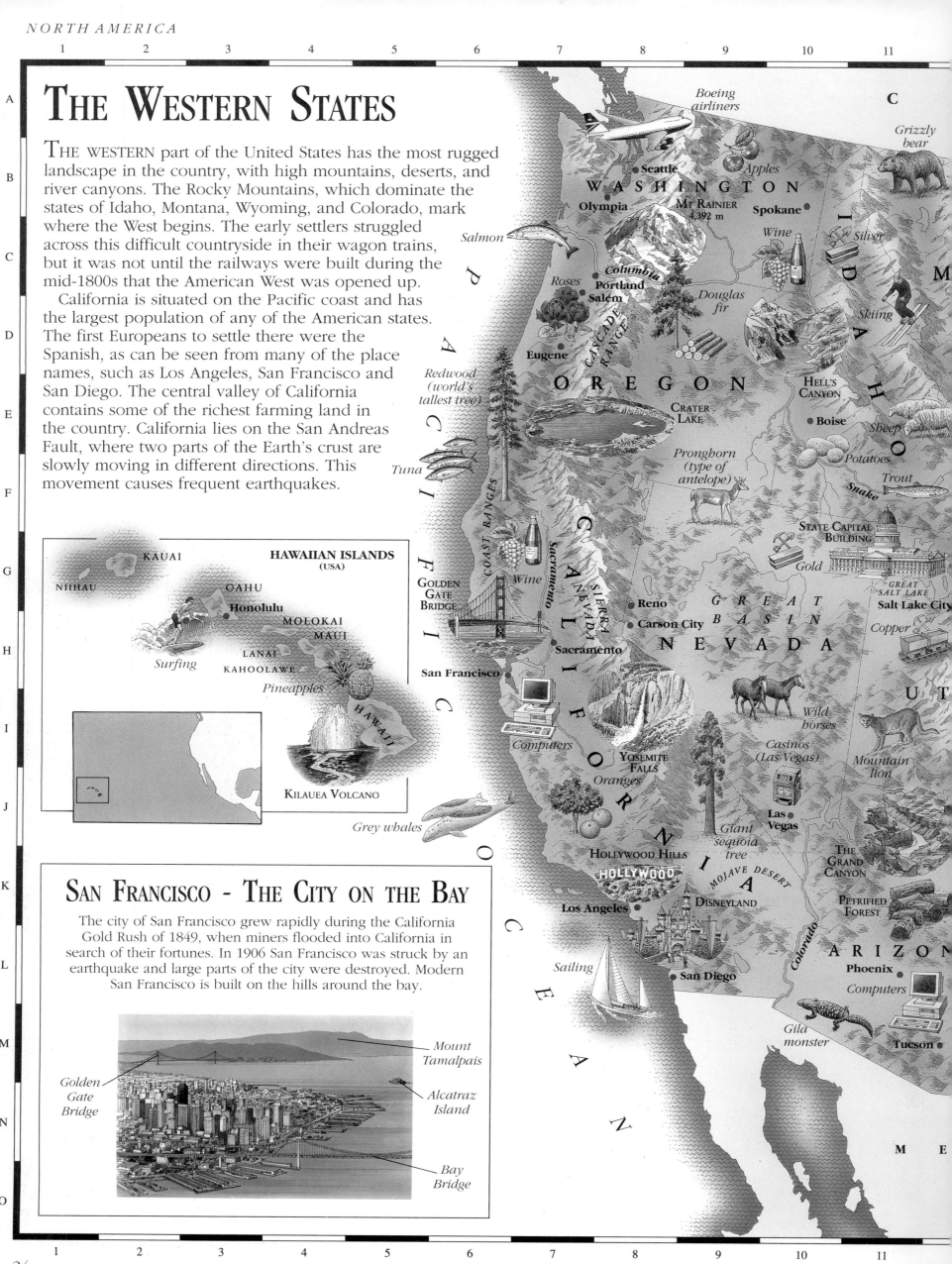

THE WESTERN STATES

THE WESTERN part of the United States has the most rugged landscape in the country, with high mountains, deserts, and river canyons. The Rocky Mountains, which dominate the states of Idaho, Montana, Wyoming, and Colorado, mark where the West begins. The early settlers struggled across this difficult countryside in their wagon trains, but it was not until the railways were built during the mid-1800s that the American West was opened up.

California is situated on the Pacific coast and has the largest population of any of the American states. The first Europeans to settle there were the Spanish, as can be seen from many of the place names, such as Los Angeles, San Francisco and San Diego. The central valley of California contains some of the richest farming land in the country. California lies on the San Andreas Fault, where two parts of the Earth's crust are slowly moving in different directions. This movement causes frequent earthquakes.

HAWAIIAN ISLANDS (USA)

KAUAI
NIIHAU
OAHU
Honolulu
MOLOKAI
MAUI
LANAI
KAHOOLAWE
Surfing
Pineapples
HAWAII
Kilauea Volcano

SAN FRANCISCO - THE CITY ON THE BAY

The city of San Francisco grew rapidly during the California Gold Rush of 1849, when miners flooded into California in search of their fortunes. In 1906 San Francisco was struck by an earthquake and large parts of the city were destroyed. Modern San Francisco is built on the hills around the bay.

Golden Gate Bridge
Mount Tamalpais
Alcatraz Island
Bay Bridge

Boeing airliners
Grizzly bear
Seattle
Apples
WASHINGTON
Olympia
Mt Rainier 4,392 m
Spokane
Salmon
Wine
Silver
IDAHO
Roses
Columbia
Portland
Salem
Douglas fir
Skiing
Eugene
OREGON
CASCADE RANGE
HELL'S CANYON
Redwood (world's tallest tree)
Crater Lake
Boise
Sheep
Pronghorn (type of antelope)
Potatoes
Tuna
Snake
Trout
STATE CAPITAL BUILDING
COAST RANGES
Wine
Sacramento
SIERRA NEVADA
Gold
GREAT SALT LAKE
GOLDEN GATE BRIDGE
Wine
Reno
GREAT BASIN
Salt Lake City
Carson City
NEVADA
Copper
San Francisco
Sacramento
Computers
Wild horses
UT
YOSEMITE FALLS
Casinos (Las Vegas)
Mountain lion
Oranges
Giant sequoia tree
Las Vegas
Grey whales
CALIFORNIA
Hollywood Hills
HOLLYWOOD
MOJAVE DESERT
THE GRAND CANYON
Los Angeles
DISNEYLAND
PETRIFIED FOREST
Sailing
ARIZON
Colorado
San Diego
Phoenix
Computers
Gila monster
Tucson

13 14 15 16 17 18 19 20 21 22 23

A N A D A

CANADA

Harvesting wheat

Wild ducks

Oil

Oil

Oil

Great Falls

Missouri

Helena

Oil

M O N T A N A

OLD FAITHFUL GEYSER (YELLOWSTONE NATIONAL PARK)

Yellowstone

N O R T H D A K O T A

Grand Forks

Bismarck

Missouri

Wheat

M I N N E S O T A

DEVIL'S TOWER

Strip-mining for coal

Sunflowers

Wapiti (type of elk)

S O U T H D A K O T A

Pierre

Beef cattle

R O C K Y

△ **GANNETT PEAK 4,207 m**

Beef cattle

W Y O M I N G

Prairie dog

Beef cattle

I O W A

Coyote (type of wild dog)

MT RUSHMORE 0,000 M

Soya beans

Missouri

Cowboy

Cheyenne

Skiing

CHIMNEY ROCK

N E B R A S K A

Wheat

Omaha

Lincoln

Green

Denver

Denver skyline

BUFFALO BILL'S RANCH HOUSE

Topeka

Kansas City

M T S

C O L O R A D O

Indian eagle dancer

MONUMENT ROCKS

K A N S A S

Oil

Aircraft industry

Wichita

RAINBOW BRIDGE

M I S S O U R I

SHIP ROCK

Rattlesnake

Oil

Oil

Sorghum (cereal crop)

Tulsa

A R K A N S A S

Saguaros (giant cacti)

Beef cattle

Santa Fe

Albuquerque

Cotton

Oil

Oklahoma City

N E W M E X I C O

Bison

O K L A H O M A

Maize

SOCORRO SPACE TELESCOPE

Rio Grande

CARLSBAD CAVERNS

T E X A S

SAN XAVIER DE BAC MISSION

X I C O

| 0 | 100 | 200 | 300 | 400 | 500 Kilometres |

| 0 | 100 | 200 | 300 Miles |

25

A
B
C
D
E
F
G
H
I
J
K
L
M
N
O

MEXICO, CENTRAL AMERICA, AND THE CARIBBEAN

CENTRAL AMERICA is a narrow land bridge that joins the two continents of North and South America. At its narrowest point, in Panama, a canal 82 km (51 miles) long has been built to join the Atlantic and Pacific oceans. There are seven small countries in Central America. To the north lies Mexico and to the east lie the hundreds of islands of the Caribbean Sea, which are often called the West Indies. This is a region of great variety and contrasts – large and small, rich and poor, old and new – with a fascinating mixture of different cultures and troubled histories. Modern Mexico City, one of the largest cities in the world,

lies on the site of an ancient city called Tenochtitlán, which was once the capital of the Aztec civilization.

On the Caribbean islands, tourist luxury and local poverty lie side by side. In the 16th century, the islands were colonized by the Europeans, who shipped black slaves from Africa to work on the farms. Today the population is a mixture of many peoples. The main languages are English, Spanish, and dialects called *patois*, which are mixtures of African and French or English.

There are also great contrasts in the climate and vegetation of this area, from the Mexican desert in the north to the rainforests of the south, and the clear blue waters and coral islands in the east. Sometimes great tropical storms called hurricanes rage through the usually calm waters of the Caribbean. Winds of over 160 kph (100 mph) and enormous waves cause much damage.

TEOTIHUACÁN

Teotihuacán, located near modern Mexico City, was the capital city of an ancient Mexican civilization. Its name means "the city of the gods". At the height of its importance, around AD 600, it had 125,000 inhabitants and covered an area of more than 20 sq km (8 sq miles). The streets were laid out in a grid pattern and were lined with temples, palaces and about 20,000 houses. The huge Pyramid of the Sun, in the middle of the city, was one of the earliest religious centres in Mexico. In about AD 750 the city was destroyed by invaders and abandoned.

MEXICO

GUATEMALA   BELIZE   HONDURAS

EL SALVADOR   NICARAGUA   COSTA RICA   PANAMA

FACTS AND FIGURES

Jamaica, which means "island of springs", is a popular tourist resort.

World's fastest population growth: The population of Central America has more than tripled since 1900.

ANTIGUA & BARBUDA
Capital: St John's

ARUBA
Capital: Oranjestad

BAHAMAS
Capital: Nassau

BARBADOS
Capital: Bridgetown

BELIZE
Capital: Belmopan

COSTA RICA
Capital: San José

CUBA
Capital: Havana

DOMINICA
Capital: Roseau

DOMINICAN REPUBLIC
Capital: Santo Domingo

EL SALVADOR
Capital: San Salvador

GRENADA
Capital: St George's

GUADELOUPE
Capital: Basse Terre

GUATEMALA
Capital: Guatemala City

HAITI
Capital: Port-au-Prince

HONDURAS
Capital: Tegucigalpa

JAMAICA
Capital: Kingston

MARTINIQUE
Capital: Fort-de-France

MEXICO
Capital: Mexico City

NETHERLANDS ANTILLES
Capital: Willemstad

NICARAGUA
Capital: Managua

PANAMA
Capital: Panama City

PUERTO RICO
Capital: San Juan

ST KITTS-NEVIS
Capital: Basseterre

ST LUCIA
Capital: Castries

ST VINCENT & THE GRENADINES
Capital: Kingstown

TRINIDAD & TOBAGO
Capital: Port-of-Spain

BAHAMAS

PUERTO RICO

BARBADOS

GRENADA

TRINIDAD & TOBAGO

CUBA

JAMAICA

HAITI

DOMINICAN REPUBLIC

ATLANTIC OCEAN

Tourism

BAHAMAS

Nassau

Cruise liner

Scuba diver

Straits of Florida

Sugar cane

Coral reefs

Coffee

TURKS & CAICOS ISLANDS (UK)

Cocoa

Coral reefs

Tourism

Frigate bird

ANGUILLA (UK)

VIRGIN ISLANDS (USA/UK)

ST KITTS-NEVIS

ANTIGUA & BARBUDA

Havana

CUBA

Pineapples

HAITI

DOMINICAN REPUBLIC

SANTO DOMINGO

San Juan

PUERTO RICO (US)

MONTSERRAT (UK)

Sailing

GUADELOUPE (Fr)

DOMINICA

Coconuts

Cigars

Port-au-Prince

Scuba diver

CAYMAN ISLANDS (UK)

JAMAICA

KINGSTON

Sharks

MARTINIQUE (Fr)

ST LUCIA

BARBADOS

Reggae music

Rum

ST VINCENT & THE GRENADINES

Nutmeg and mace

Green turtle

CARIBBEAN SEA

GRENADA

Steel bands

TRINIDAD & TOBAGO

Grapefruit

HONDURAS

Cattle

TEGUCIGALPA

Coffee

ARUBA (Neth)

NETHERLANDS ANTILLES

Bananas

NICARAGUA

MANAGUA

Coffee

PANAMA CANAL

COLOMBIA

VENEZUELA

SAN JOSE

COSTA RICA

Toucan

PANAMA

PANAMA CITY

Spider monkey

0	200	400	600	800 Kilometres

0	100	200	300	400	500 Miles

SOUTH AMERICA

THE CONTINENT of South America is made up of great mountain ranges, thick forests, wide plains, and deserts. Running from north to south down the western side of South America are the snow-capped peaks of the Andes. These mountains are amongst the most recently formed on Earth and in places they are still slowly rising. Along the range of mountains are hundreds of volcanoes, some of which are still active. Many of the streams and rivers which join together to form the mighty Amazon river start in the Andes. The Amazon basin, which lies across the Equator, is a hot, wet region which contains the largest tropical rainforest in the world.

The flat, fertile grasslands of the Pampas in the southeast of the continent are used for rearing cattle on huge farms called ranches, and for growing wheat. Farther south lies the colder, desert landscape of Patagonia. At the tip of the continent is Cape Horn, for centuries feared by sailors because fierce storms rage there for much of the year.

Peruvians in national costume.

In 1498 Christopher Columbus became the first European to see the coast of South America. Europeans quickly colonized the continent, and until the beginning of the 19th century South America was ruled by Spain and Portugal. Argentina was the first country to gain its independence, in 1816. The people of South America are descended from American Indians, Europeans, and Africans. Spanish is the main language, except in Brazil, where Portuguese is spoken. Many Indians speak their own languages.

About half of South America's people make their living from farming. Most farmers grow just enough beans or corn for their families to live on, but there are large plantations where coffee, sugar-cane, wheat, and other crops are grown. South America is also rich in natural resources, such as oil, gold, silver, copper, iron, tin, and lead.

Saw mill on the Amazon River.

Ancient Inca city at Machu Picchu, Peru.

FACTS ABOUT SOUTH AMERICA

Area: 17,835,000 sq km (6,886,000 sq miles).

Population: 309,684,500.

Number of independent countries: 12.

Largest countries: Brazil, 8,511,965 sq km (3,286,726 sq miles); Argentina, 2,776,889 sq km (1,068,304 sq miles).

Most populated countries: Brazil, 156,600,000; Argentina, 33,500,000.

Largest metropolitan areas: São Paulo (Brazil), 15,199,500; Rio de Janeiro (Brazil), 9,600,600; Buenos Aires (Argentina), 9,927,400.

Highest mountains: Aconcagua (Argentina), 6,960 m (22,834 ft), the world's highest extinct volcano; Ojos del Salado (Argentina-Chile), 6,908 m (22,664 ft), the world's highest active volcano; Bonete (Argentina), 6,872 m (22,546 ft).

Longest rivers: Amazon, 6,437 km (4,000 miles); Paraná, 4,500 km (2,796 miles); Madeira, 3,199 km (1,988 miles); São Francisco, 3,199 km (1,988 miles); Purús, 2,993 km (1,860 miles).

Main deserts: Atacama (Chile), about 132,000 sq km (50,965 sq miles); Patagonia (Argentina), about 770,000 sq km (300,000 sq miles).

Largest forest area: Amazon basin, about 7,000,000 sq km (2,700,000 sq miles).

Largest lake: Lake Titicaca (Peru-Bolivia), 8,340 sq km (3,220 sq miles). Titicaca is also the highest navigable lake in the world.

Largest island: Tierra del Fuego (Chile-Argentina), 47,000 km (18,140 sq miles).

World's wettest place: Tutunendo (Colombia) has an average annual rainfall of 11,770 mm (463.4 in).

World's driest place: Parts of the Atacama Desert (Chile) have an average annual rainfall of nil. In 1971 rain fell there for the first time in over 400 years.

World's highest waterfall: Angel Falls on the River Carrao (Venezuela) has a total drop of 979 m (3,212 ft).

World's largest lagoon: Lagoa dos Patos (Brazil) covers 10,645 sq km (4,110 sq miles).

Map labels

PACIFIC OCEAN

ATLANTIC OCEAN

VENEZUELA

COLOMBIA

GUYANA

SURINAM

FRENCH GUIANA

ECUADOR

PERU

BRAZIL

BOLIVIA

PARAGUAY

CHILE

ARGENTINA

URUGUAY

FALKLAND ISLANDS (UK)

P

NORTH AMERICA

ATLANTIC OCEAN

GULF OF MEXICO

GREATER ANTILLES

LESSER ANTILLES

CARIBBEAN SEA

CENTRAL AMERICA

GULF OF PANAMA

LAKE MARACAIBO

Orinoco

AFRICA

GUIANA HIGHLANDS

MARAJÓ ISLAND

GALÁPAGOS ISLANDS

Negro

Amazon

AMAZON BASIN

Tocantins

Parnaíba

PACIFIC OCEAN

A N D E S

△ Huascarán 6,768 m

Purus

Madeira

São Francisco

MATO GROSSO

BRAZILIAN HIGHLANDS

LAKE TITICACA

GRAN CHACO

Paraguay

Parana

TRINIDADE

LAKE POOPÓ

ATACAMA DESERT

Ojos del Salado 6,908 m
△ Bonete 6,872 m

Parana

Uruguay

LAGOA DOS PATOS

A N D E S

△ Aconcagua 6,960 m

PAMPAS

RIVER PLATE

BAHIA BLANCA

TRISTAN DA CUNHA

PATAGONIA

GULF OF ST MATÍAS

FALKLAND ISLANDS (ISLAS MALVINAS)

SOUTH GEORGIA

TIERRA DEL FUEGO

CAPE HORN

DRAKE PASSAGE

SOUTH SHETLAND ISLANDS

SOUTH SANDWICH ISLANDS

ANTARCTICA

NORTHERN SOUTH AMERICA

THE NORTHERN PART of South America is dominated by the vast, humid Amazon rainforest and by the high, snow-capped Andes mountains in the west. The Amazon river is the second longest in the world, after the Nile, and runs for 6,437 km (4,000 miles) from its source in the Peruvian Andes to its mouth in northern Brazil. Every hour the Amazon delivers an average of 773 billion litres (170 billion gallons) of water into the Atlantic.

The Andes region of Peru was the centre of the great Inca empire, which flourished in the 15th and 16th centuries. It was destroyed in 1532-33 by the Spanish conquistadors, led by Francisco Pizarro. The Incas were brilliant engineers, building roads and canals through difficult mountain landscapes. They were also skilled scientists, craftsmen, and farmers.

Brazil is by far the largest country in South America, both in size and population. In the over-crowded cities of southeast Brazil, such as São Paulo and Rio de Janeiro, large numbers of poor people live in slums known as "favelas".

In recent years, political and social problems have caused much upheaval in this region. Some of the nations are ruled by dictators. Colombia is one of the most dangerous countries in the world because of its ruthless drug trade. Tourism, however, remains an important source of income in South America.

COLOMBIA

ECUADOR

PERU

BOLIVIA

PACIFIC OCEAN

Barranquilla
Cartagena
PANAMA
Emeralds
Medellín
Manizales
Cali
Bananas
Panama hat
Coffee
Quito
ECUADOR
COTOPAXI 5,897 m
Piura
Chiclayo
Trujillo
HUASCARÁN 6,768 m △
LIMA
Bogotá Cathedral
BOGOTÁ
Harpy eagle
Coffee
Pre-Columbian stone idol
Iquitos
Cavies (guinea pigs)
Indian flute players
Llama
Rubber trees
ANDES MTS
PERU
MACHU PICCHU (INCA CITY)
LAKE TITICACA
Andean condor
Arequipa
Reed boat on Lake Titicaca

Scarlet Ibis
Pearls
CARACAS
Valencia
Oil
Oil
Barquisimeto
Ciudad Bolívar
VENEZUELA
Oil
Oil
Oil
Diamonds
Orinoco
ANGEL FALLS
Red howler monkey
Jaguar
Negro
Capybara (world's largest rodent)
Peruvian cock-of-the-rock
Indian hunter
Humming bird
Purús
Toco toucan
Rainforest
Madeira
Pôrto Velho
Two-toed sloth
Spectacled bear
ILLIMANI 6,402 m △
LA PAZ
BOLIVIA
Cochabamba
Sucre
Santa Cruz
Bolivian Indian
Puya raimondii (world's tallest herb)

THE AMAZON RAINFOREST

The Amazon rainforest covers an area larger than Western Europe and supports more than one-fifth of the world's plant and animal species. It is also the home of tribes of Indians who have lived there for thousands of years. But each year about 200,000 sq km (77,200 sq miles) of forest is cut down for farming and mining. As a result of deforestation, many of the plants and animals are disappearing.

GALAPAGOS ISLANDS
(ECUADOR)

Marine iguana
Galapagos giant tortoise
ISABELA ISLAND

0   50   100 Kilometres
0   25   50   75 Miles

VENEZUELA

GUYANA

SURINAM

FRENCH GUIANA

0   200   400   600   800   1000 Kilometres

0   150   300   450   600 Miles

A T L A N T I C

O C E A N

GEORGETOWN

ARIANE ROCKET
LAUNCH SITE

PARAMARIBO

Sugar cane

CAYENNE

G
U
Y
A
N
A

SURINAM

F
R
E
N
C
H

G
U
I
A
N
A

Wayana Indian

*Water
buffalo*

Green turtle

Lobster

MANAUS
OPERA
HOUSE

Amazon

MARAJÓ
ISLAND

Belém

*Coconut
palms*

BRAZIL

*Jangada
fishing raft*

Manaus

*Gold and
blue macaw*

*Mango
tree*

Gold

Xingu

Anaconda

*Kayapo
Indian*

Brazil nuts

Fortaleza

Bananas

Tourism

Caiman

Teresina

Natal

*Suya
Indian*

Tapir

Tocantins

Araguaia

São Francisco

CHURCH OF
OUR LADY OF
CARMO

Recife

*Umbrella
bird*

B R A Z I L

Tourism

*Giant
armadillo*

BRAZILIA
CATHEDRAL
DOME

*Sugar
cane*

Marmoset

M A T O
G R O S S O

Salvador

*Cocoa
pods*

A

Cuiabá

Brasília

Cattle

Gold

Shrimps

Football

**Campo
Grande**

Coffee

Humming bird

Tourism

Carnival

Belo Horizonte

*Jabiru
stork*

Wheat

CORCOVADO
STATUE OF CHRIST

Campinas

**Rio de
Janeiro**

Cars

São Paulo

Tourism

Curitiba

SUGAR LOAF MT
395 m

*Gaucho
(cattleherder)*

Paraná

Hake

PÔRTO ALEGRE
CATHEDRAL

**Pôrto
Alegre**

Soya beans

FACTS AND FIGURES

Traditional reed boats are still used on Lake Titicaca, the highest navigable lake in the world.

Highest mountains:
Huascarán (Peru), 6,768 m (22,205 ft); Illimani (Bolivia), 6,402 m (21,004 ft).

Longest rivers:
Amazon, 6,437 km (4,000 miles); Madeira, 3,199 km (1,988 miles); São Francisco, 3,199 km (1,988 miles); Purús, 2,993 km (1,860 miles).

Largest lake: Lake Titicaca (Peru-Bolivia), 8,340 sq km (3,220 sq miles).

World's highest waterfall: Angel Falls (Venezuela), 979 m (3,212 ft).

Largest metropolitan areas:
São Paulo (Brazil), 15,199,500; Rio de Janeiro (Brazil), 9,600,600; Lima (Peru), 6,483,900.

World's leading coffee grower:
Brazil grows around 4,000,000 tonnes (3,936,826 tons) of coffee each year.

Sugar Loaf Mountain stands at the entrance to the harbour in Rio de Janeiro, one of Brazil's major ports.

BOLIVIA
Capital: La Paz
Area: 1,098,581 sq km (424,195 sq miles)
Population: 7,700,000

BRAZIL
Capital: Brasília
Area: 8,511,965 sq km (3,286,726 sq miles)
Population: 156,600,000

COLOMBIA
Capital: Bogotá
Area: 1,138,914 sq km (439,770 sq miles)
Population: 34,000,000

ECUADOR
Capital: Quito
Area: 283,561 sq km (109,526 sq miles)
Population: 11,300,000

FRENCH GUIANA
Capital: Cayenne
Area: 90,000 sq km (34,751 sq miles)
Population: 118,000

GUYANA
Capital: Georgetown
Area: 214,969 sq km (82,980 sq miles)
Population: 800,000

PERU
Capital: Lima
Area: 1,285,216 sq km (496,260 sq miles)
Population: 22,900,000

SURINAM
Capital: Paramaribo
Area: 163,265 sq km (63,041 sq miles)
Population: 400,000

VENEZUELA
Capital: Caracas
Area: 912,050 sq km (352,170 sq miles)
Population: 20,600,000

SOUTHERN SOUTH AMERICA

THE TWO LARGEST COUNTRIES in southern South America are Argentina and Chile. Their people are mainly of European descent. The landscape in Argentina varies dramatically, from the Andes mountains to forests, grassy plains and the bare, windswept plateau of Patagonia. The country is rich in mineral deposits, such as oil, natural gas, coal, and iron ore, but its most important natural resource is the Pampas – a fertile, grassy plain where large numbers of cattle are reared. Argentina is one of the world's main exporters of beef.

Chile is a long, thin strip of land stretching about 4,200 km (2,610 miles) from Peru to Punta Arenas, one of the southernmost cities in the world. Separated from the rest of South America by the Andes, Chile has many kinds of climate, from the Atacama Desert in the north, to ice and glaciers in the south. Chile has huge deposits of minerals, such as copper, iron ore and nitrates, which account for much of its wealth.

In the countries of Paraguay and Uruguay most people make their living from agriculture, especially raising sheep and cattle. Paraguay is among the world's poorer countries – most farmers there grow just enough to support their families. The Falkland Islands, which are governed by the United Kingdom, lie in the Atlantic Ocean about 500 km (310 miles) off the coast of Argentina. They are surrounded by rich fishing grounds and oil reserves. The islands are also claimed by the Argentinians, who call them the *Islas Malvinas*. Most people in the Falkland Islands make their living from sheep farming.

Map labels

BRAZIL

PARAGUAY

Oranges

Paraná

IGUAÇU FALLS

Tobacco

URUGUAY

Gaucho (cattleherder)

Paraná

Paraguay

ASUNCIÓN

Cotton

Paraguay

Corrientes

Sheep

MONTEVIDEO

Concepción

Cotton

Carreta (ox-drawn cart)

Resistencia

Maté (type of tea)

RIVER PLATE

Cattle

PARAGUAY

Salado

Cattle

Paraná

BUENOS AIRES

La Plata

GRAN CHACO

Paraná

Tango dancers

Quebracho tree

Santa Fe

COLON OPERA HOUSE

BOLIVIA

Giant ant-eater

San Miguel de Tucumán

Football

Córdoba

Rhea

Cattle

Santiago del Estero

Sugar cane

Rosario

PAMPAS

Wine

Polo players

Gaucho (cattleherder)

Prickly pear

ARGENTINA

PERU

ANDES

Atuel

Vicuña (type of llama)

Alpaca

San Juan

MT ACONCAGUA 6,960 m

Mendoza

Wine

LICANCÁBUR VOLCANO 5,921 m

A OJOS DEL SALADO 6,908 m

Wine

Copper

ATACAMA DESERT

Iron

Andean condor

Cherries

Viña del Mar

SANTIAGO

Skiing

Arica

Iquique

Rancagua

Valparaíso

Wine

Antofagasta

CHILE

Flags

PARAGUAY

ARGENTINA

CHILE

URUGUAY

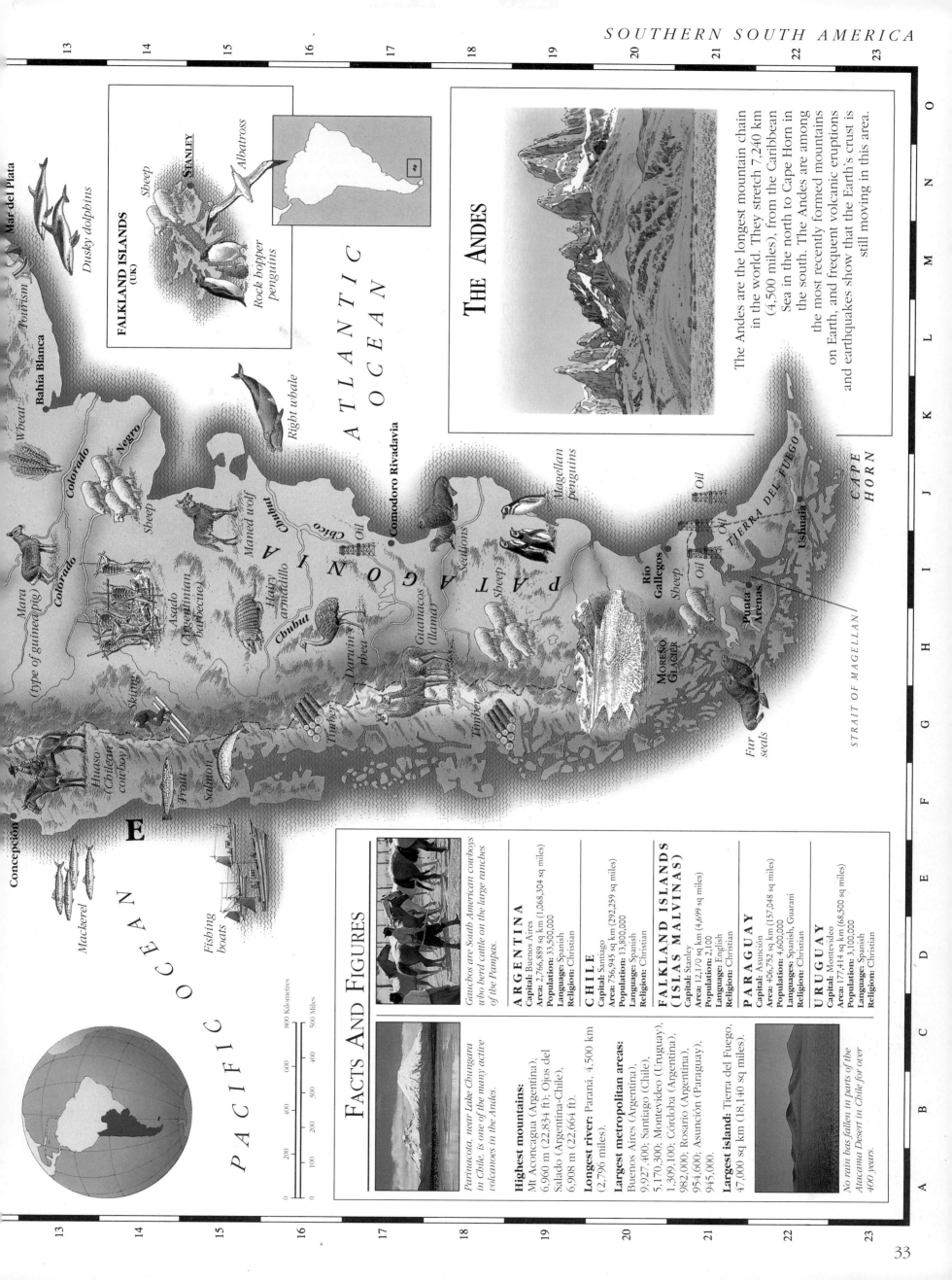

FALKLAND ISLANDS
(UK)

STANLEY

Albatross

Sheep

Rock hopper penguins

THE ANDES

The Andes are the longest mountain chain in the world. They stretch 7,240 km (4,500 miles), from the Caribbean Sea in the north to Cape Horn in the south. The Andes are among the most recently formed mountains on Earth, and frequent volcanic eruptions and earthquakes show that the Earth's crust is still moving in this area.

Mar del Plata

Dusky dolphins

Tourism

Bahía Blanca

Wheat

Right whale

A T L A N T I C   O C E A N

Negro

Colorado

Colorado

Sheep

Maned wolf

Mara (type of guineapig)

Asado (Argentinian barbecue)

Colorado

Hairy armadillo

Chubut

Chubut

P A T A G O N I A

Chico

Oil

Comodoro Rivadavia

Magellan penguins

Sea lions

Sheep

Darwin's rhea

Guanacos (llama)

Timber

Oil

Rio Gallegos

MORENO GLACIER

TIERRA DEL FUEGO

Oil

Oil

Punta Arenas

Sheep

Ushuaia

C A P E   H O R N

Fur seals

STRAIT OF MAGELLAN

Concepción

Skiing

Huaso (Chilean cowboy)

Trout

Salmon

E

Mackerel

Fishing boats

P A C I F I C   O C E A N

800 Kilometres
500 Miles

FACTS AND FIGURES

Gauchos are South American cowboys who herd cattle on the large ranches of the Pampas.

ARGENTINA
Capital: Buenos Aires
Area: 2,766,889 sq km (1,068,304 sq miles)
Population: 33,500,000
Language: Spanish
Religion: Christian

CHILE
Capital: Santiago
Area: 756,945 sq km (292,259 sq miles)
Population: 13,800,000
Language: Spanish
Religion: Christian

FALKLAND ISLANDS (ISLAS MALVINAS)
Capital: Stanley
Area: 12,170 sq km (4,699 sq miles)
Population: 2,100
Language: English
Religion: Christian

PARAGUAY
Capital: Asunción
Area: 406,752 sq km (157,048 sq miles)
Population: 4,600,000
Languages: Spanish, Guarani
Religion: Christian

URUGUAY
Capital: Montevideo
Area: 177,414 sq km (68,500 sq miles)
Population: 3,100,000
Language: Spanish
Religion: Christian

Parinacota, near Lake Chungara in Chile, is one of the many active volcanoes in the Andes.

Highest mountains:
Mt Aconcagua (Argentina), 6,960 m (22,834 ft): Ojos del Salado (Argentina-Chile), 6,908 m (22,664 ft).

Longest river: Paraná, 4,500 km (2,796 miles).

Largest metropolitan areas:
Buenos Aires (Argentina), 9,927,400; Santiago (Chile), 5,170,300; Montevideo (Uruguay), 1,309,100; Córdoba (Argentina), 982,000; Rosario (Argentina), 954,600; Asunción (Paraguay), 945,000.

Largest island: Tierra del Fuego, 47,000 sq km (18,140 sq miles).

No rain has fallen in parts of the Atacama Desert in Chile for over 400 years.

EUROPE

The headquarters of the EC in Brussels, Belgium.

EUROPE IS THE SECOND smallest continent by area, but it has the second largest population of all the seven continents. Europe is bounded by the Atlantic and Arctic Oceans in the north and west, and in the south by the Mediterranean Sea. Europe's only land frontier is marked by the Ural and Caucasus mountains in the Russian Federation.

The landscape of Europe is very varied. In southern Europe, much of the land is hilly or mountainous. The history of this region has been greatly influenced by the Mediterranean Sea, which for centuries has been a vital trade route between Europe, Africa, and Asia.

The northern and southern parts of mainland Europe are divided by the Alps, the highest range of mountains in western Europe. The landscape of northern Europe is generally flat and is dominated by the North European Plain, which stretches from the Atlantic coast right across to the Ural Mountains. In the far north of the continent lie the mainly mountainous countries of Scandinavia.

In 1945, after the end of the Second World War, the European countries were divided into two groups – the West and East. The border between them was sometimes described as an Iron Curtain because few people were allowed to cross it.

The Eastern European countries were Romania, Poland, Yugoslavia, Czechoslovakia, Hungary, Bulgaria, Albania, and East Germany. Until the late 1980s, these countries had communist governments and many of them were closely linked to the former USSR. But in recent years, there have been dramatic changes in this area. Almost all the Eastern European countries have abandoned communism, and many new countries have been formed in the region. East and West Germany reunited in 1990. Latvia, Lithuania, Estonia, Belorussia, Ukraine, and Moldavia all became independent countries in 1991 when the USSR split up. Croatia, Slovenia, Bosnia and Herzegovina, and Macedonia broke away from Yugoslavia in 1992, and in 1993 Czechoslovakia split into two countries – the Czech Republic and Slovakia.

Lavender fields in France.

The Western European nations are among the richest countries in the world. Twelve countries in Western Europe have joined together to form the European Community (EC). The member states are Austria, Belgium, Denmark, Finland, France, Germany, Greece, Ireland, Italy, Luxembourg, the Netherlands, Portugal, Spain, Sweden, and the UK. The aim of the EC is to unite the economic resources of its members into a single economy.

During the 18th and 19th centuries Western European countries became the first nations in the world to have industrial revolutions. They changed from farming to manufacturing and exporting industrial goods. Europe still has the greatest concentration of industry of all the continents, but many Europeans still make their living from farming.

Vegetable market in Montenegro, Yugoslavia.

FACTS ABOUT EUROPE

Area: 10,498,000 sq km (4,053,309 sq miles). This is seven per cent of the world's total land area.

Population: 770,568,400 (including the European part of the Russian Federation). This is nearly 14 per cent of the world's total population.

Number of countries: 44 (this includes 3 per cent of Turkey and 25 per cent of the Russian Federation).

Largest countries: Russian Federation - the European part of the Russian Federation covers 4,551,000 sq km (1,757,000 sq miles), this is only 28 per cent of the total area of the Russian Federation; France, 551,500 sq km (212,936 sq miles).

Most populated countries: Russian Federation - 114,412,000 people live in the European part of the Russian Federation; Germany, 77,714,000.

Largest metropolitan areas: Moscow (Russian Federation), 8,957,000; London (UK), 6,679,700; Paris (France), 9,318,900; St. Petersburg (Russian Federation), 5,004,000; Essen (Germany), 626,100..

Highest mountains: Elbrus (Russian Federation), 5,642 m (18,510 ft); Mont Blanc (France-Italy), 4,807 m (15,770 ft); Monte Rosa (Italy-Switzerland), 4,634 m (15,203ft).

A
B
C
D

L
M
N
O

NORTH AMERICA

ARCTIC
OCEAN

GREENLAND

FRANZ
JOSEF LAND

SVALBARD

NOVAYA ZEMLYA

BARENTS
SEA

NORWEGIAN
SEA

ICELAND

KJØLEN MTS

LAKE
ONEGA

LAKE
LADOGA

URAL MTS

A S I A

FAEROE
ISLANDS

BRITISH
ISLES

NORTH
SEA

BALTIC SEA

Elbe

Rhine

CENTRAL
RUSSIAN
UPLANDS

AZORES

BAY OF
BISCAY

NORTH EUROPEAN PLAIN

Dnieper

Don

Volga

PYRENEES

Rhône

ALPS

Po

CARPATHIANS

CAUCASUS

CASPIAN SEA

Tagus

APENNINES

HUNGARIAN
PLAIN

Danube

MADEIRA

CORSICA

BLACK SEA

CANARY
ISLANDS

BALEARIC
ISLANDS

SARDINIA

MEDITERRANEAN SEA

SICILY

CRETE

CYPRUS

AFRICA

ARABIAN
PENINSULA

RED SEA

OCEAN

INDIAN OCEAN

THE BRITISH ISLES

THE BRITISH ISLES lie off the northwestern coast of mainland Europe. They consist of two large islands – Great Britain and Ireland – surrounded by many smaller ones. The British Isles are divided into two countries: the United Kingdom and Ireland. The United Kingdom, which is often known as Britain, is itself made up of England, Wales, Scotland, and Northern Ireland.

During the 18th and 19th centuries, the United Kingdom was the first country in the world to undergo an industrial revolution. It became the world's leading manufacturing and trading nation. During this period, Britain acquired an enormous empire, covering more than a quarter of the world. Britain's colonies included Canada, Australia, New Zealand, India, and much of Africa. During the 20th century, almost all of these colonies have become independent, although they remain linked with Britain through the Commonwealth, which has 50 member countries. Today, the United Kingdom is a member of the European Community.

Until this century, Ireland was part of the United Kingdom. In 1921 the southern part of Ireland became an independent country. Most people in the south are Roman Catholic. The northern part of Ireland, where the people are mainly Protestant, remained part of the United Kingdom. The division of Ireland has caused the violent clashes which have taken place in Northern Ireland in recent years.

FACTS AND FIGURES

Much of Ireland's wealth comes from farming, particularly raising cattle and sheep.

Largest metropolitan areas:
Dublin, 915,600; Cork, 174,400; Limerick, 75,500.

Highest mountain:
Carrauntoohil, 1,038 m (3,415 ft).

Longest river: Shannon, 386 km (240 miles).

IRELAND
Capital: Dublin
Area: 70,284 sq km (27,136 sq miles)
Population: 3,500,000
Languages: English, Irish
Religion: Christian
Currency: Punt (Irish pound)
Government: Republic

FACTS AND FIGURES

The mountainous area of Snowdonia, in northern Wales, is popular for hill walking and mountaineering.

Largest metropolitan areas:
London (England), 6,679,700; Manchester (England), 2,775,000; Birmingham (England), 2,551,700.

Highest mountains: Ben Nevis (Scotland), 1,343 m (4,406 ft); Snowdon (Wales), 1,085 m (3,560 ft).

Longest rivers:
Severn (England-Wales), 354 km (220 miles); Thames (England), 346 km (215 miles).

World's longest bridge span:
The Humber Bridge, in England, is 1,410 m (4,626 ft) long.

The traditional centre of an English country town or village is its parish church.

UNITED KINGDOM
Capital: London
Area: 244,017 sq km (94,215 sq miles)
Population: 57,800,000
Language: English
Religion: Christian
Currency: Pound sterling
Government: Monarchy

ENGLAND
Capital: London
Area: 130,360 sq km (50,332 sq miles)
Population: 48,071,300

NORTHERN IRELAND
Capital: Belfast
Area: 14,121 sq km (5,452 sq miles)
Population: 1,643,400

SCOTLAND
Capital: Edinburgh
Area: 78,769 sq km (30,412 sq miles)
Population: 5,148,600

WALES
Capital: Cardiff
Area: 20,767 sq km (8,018 sq miles)
Population: 2,936,800

UNITED KINGDOM

SHETLAND ISLANDS

Lerwick

Crofting (farming)

Pilchard

Seals

Cod

ORKNEY ISLANDS

Haddock

LEWIS

NORTH UIST

SOUTH UIST

SKYE

MULL

ISLAY

ARRAN

H E B R I D E S

Making Harris tweed

Sheep

Red deer

Salmon

A T L A N T I C   O C E A N

Fish packing

Aberdeen

Oil rig

Fishing trawler

Chemicals

Newcastle upon Tyne

Highland dress

Whisky

BALMORAL CASTLE

BEN NEVIS 1343 m

THE LOCH NESS MONSTER

Machinery

LOCH LOMOND

Edinburgh

EDINBURGH CASTLE

Glasgow

Golf

Sheep

Shipbuilding

S C O T L A N D

Highland cattle

GIANT'S CAUSEWAY

Londonderry

NORTHERN IRELAND

Carlisle

Textiles

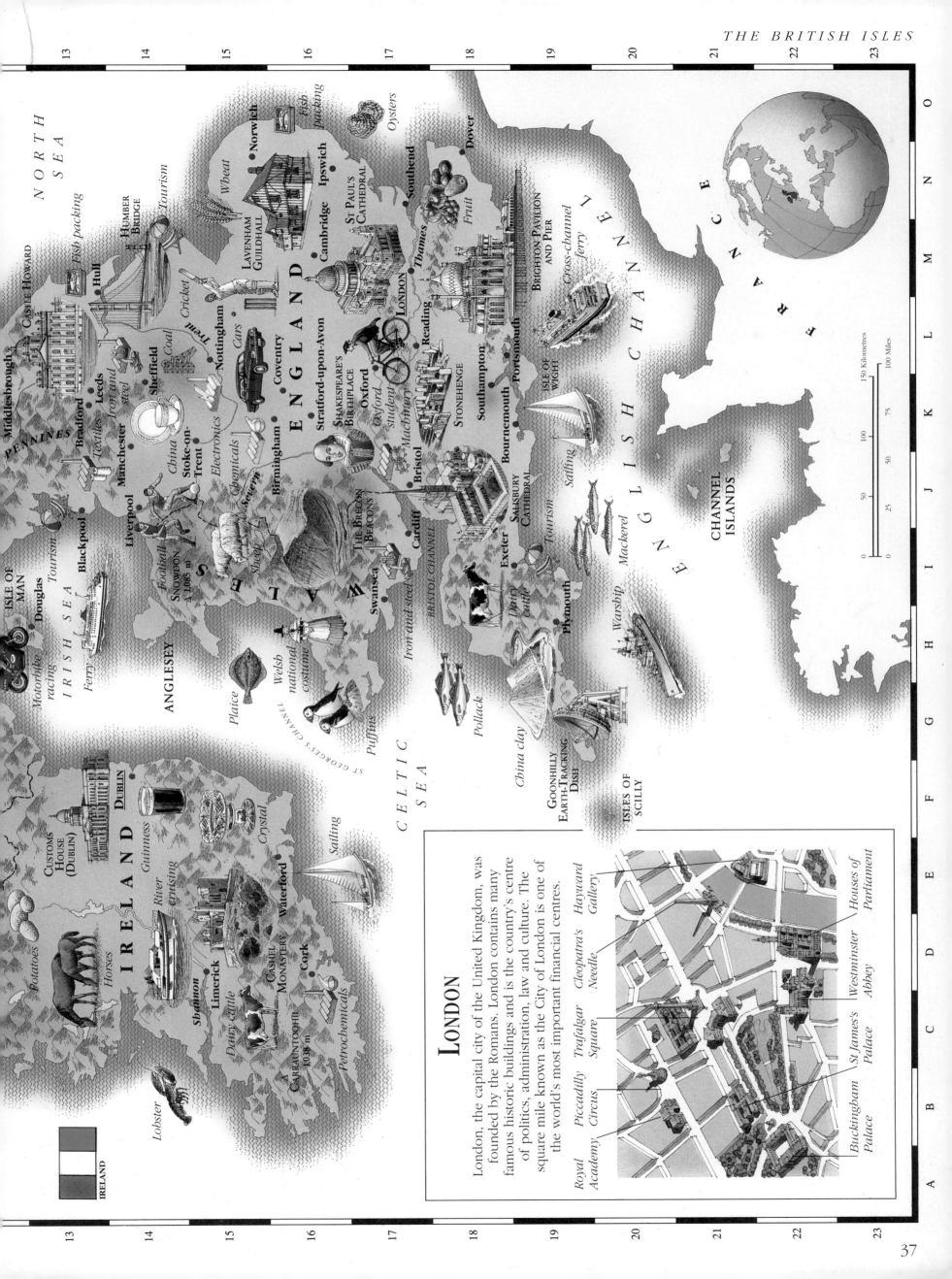

LONDON

London, the capital city of the United Kingdom, was founded by the Romans. London contains many famous historic buildings and is the country's centre of politics, administration, law and culture. The square mile known as the City of London is one of the world's most important financial centres.

FRANCE

FRANCE is one of Europe's major farming and industrial nations and is famous for the food and wine it produces. The landscape in France varies dramatically from region to region and includes rich farmland, hot, dry areas, snow-capped mountains, and large forests.

France has always been an important European power. In 1789 the French overthrew their king, Louis XVI, during the French Revolution. After the revolution, Napoleon, a general in the French army, seized power and crowned himself Emperor. He went on to conquer most of mainland Europe, but was defeated at the Battle of Waterloo in 1815. During the 19th century, French explorers and soldiers won a large colonial empire in Africa and Asia.

Today France is one of the world's leading manufacturing countries, with large iron, steel, chemical, car, aeroplane, and textile industries. France is also rich in farming land. Its major crops include barley, oats, wheat, flax, sugar beet, and grapes. Dairy farming is widespread and French farmers produce over 700 different types of cheese.

Tourism is another important source of wealth. There are many resorts around the coasts of France, and the Alps and Pyrenees are popular for winter sports.

PARIS

Visitors from all over the world flock to Paris to see its many famous sights, including the Eiffel Tower, the Arc de Triomphe, the artists' quarter of Montmartre, the tree-lined avenues, or *boulevards*, and the museums and art galleries. Paris is built on both sides of the River Seine and on two islands – the Ile St Louis and the Ile de la Cité. On the Right Bank of the river are the capital's smart shops and fashion houses. The many pavement cafés and bookshops on the Left Bank, or Latin Quarter, attract students and artists.

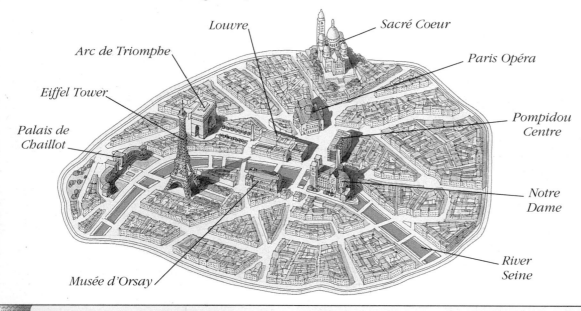

Louvre
Sacré Coeur
Arc de Triomphe
Paris Opéra
Eiffel Tower
Palais de Chaillot
Pompidou Centre
Notre Dame
River Seine
Musée d'Orsay

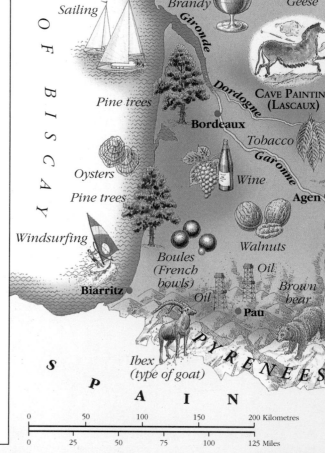

B E L G I U M

G E R M A N Y

LUXEMBOURG

Dunkirk
Calais
Lille
Tourism
Somme
Amiens
AMIENS CATHEDRAL
Beef cattle
Fashion design
Cars
WORLD WAR I MEMORIAL (VIMY)
CHÂTEAU BAS (SEDAN)
Coal
Reims
CHÂTEAU DE PIERREFONDS
Paris
Wheat
Seine
Metz
Champagne
Potatoes
Nancy
Pigs
Wild boar
Strasbourg
Coal
Wine
Storks
Mulhouse
CHARTRES CATHEDRAL
Orléans
Loire
SAINTE MADELEINE (VÉZELAY)
Mustard
CHAPEL OF NOTRE DAME DU HAUT
V O S G E S
Wine
Dijon
Beaune
J U R A
CHÂTEAU DE CHAMBORD
CHÂTEAUNEUF (NIÈVRE)
Loire
Saône
Wine
Deer
S W I T Z E R L A N D
A N C E
Porcelain
Mâcon
TGV (high-speed train)
Wine
Rhône
MONT BLANC 4,807 m
I T A L Y
Limoges
Hunting for truffles
Clermont-Ferrand
Lyon
St Etienne
Skiing
M A S S I F C E N T R A L
Cycling
CHAPEL OF ST MICHEL D'AIGUILHE (LE PUY)
Grenoble
Wine
Mountain climbing
Chamois (type of goat)
A L P S
C E V E N N E S
Rhône
Sheep
Snails
PONT VALENTRE (CAHORS)
Garonne
Aircraft industry
Montpellier
AMPHITHEATRE AT ARLES
Olives
Lavender
Tourism
MONACO
Nice
Cannes
Tourism
WALLED TOWN (CARCASSONNE)
Toulouse
Tourism
Marseille
Toulon
Fishing
S E A
Flamingos
Sailing
Warship
SOLAR FURNACE (ODEILLO)
Wine
Sardines
M E D I T E R R A N E A N

MONACO

FACTS AND FIGURES

Amboise is one of the many historic towns along the River Loire in western France.

Highest mountains:
Mont Blanc, 4,807 m (15,770 ft); Les Ecrins, 4,103m (13,461 ft); Pic de Vignemale, 3,298 m (10,820 ft); Mont Dore, 1,886 m (6,188 ft).

Longest rivers:
Loire, 1,005 km (625 miles); Rhône-Saône, 812 km (505 miles); Seine, 775 km (481 miles).

Largest metropolitan areas:
Paris, 9,318,900; Lyon, 1,262,300; Marseille, 1,231,000; Lille, 959,300; Bordeaux, 969,400.

The TGV, which runs between Paris and Lyon, is one of the world's fastest trains, with a top speed of 270 kph (168 mph).

FRANCE
Capital: Paris
Area: 551,500 sq km (212,936 sq miles)
Population: 57,400,000
Language: French
Religion: Christian
Currency: French franc

MONACO
Capital: Monaco
Area: 1.6 sq km (0.6 sq miles)
Population: 28,000
Language: French
Religion: Christian
Currency: French franc

Sunflowers are grown all over southern France. Their seeds are used to make cooking oil.

CORSICA (FRANCE)

Bastia
Tourism
C O R S I C A
Ajaccio
Tourism

BELGIUM, THE NETHERLANDS, AND LUXEMBOURG

BELGIUM, THE NETHERLANDS, AND LUXEMBOURG are situated on the North European Plain, where much of the land is very flat and low lying. For this reason, they are often called the "Low Countries". The only area of higher land in the region is the hilly Ardennes forest in southern Belgium and Luxembourg.

Almost half of the Netherlands lies below sea level. There is a saying that "God made the world, but the Dutch made the Netherlands", because over the centuries the Dutch have reclaimed large areas of land from the sea. The reclaimed land, called a polder, is drained and then protected against flooding with long walls called dykes.

Belgium, the Netherlands, and Luxembourg are sometimes called "Benelux", which is a shortened version of the three country names. Although these countries are small, they have large populations. The Netherlands has one of the highest concentrations of people in Europe – an average of 360 people live in each square kilometre of land. All three Benelux countries have successful industrial economies. Farming is also important, and the most up-to-date methods are used. The main products are livestock, dairy produce, fruit, vegetables, and flowers. Fishing and tourism are also important sources of income. Belgium and the Netherlands have been important trading nations for many centuries. Today, Rotterdam in the Netherlands and Antwerp in Belgium are the two busiest ports in Europe.

The Benelux countries are members of the European Community, which has its headquarters in Brussels, the Belgian capital. Luxembourg is a centre for European organizations, while the International Courts of Justice are situated at The Hague in the Netherlands.

Map labels

THE NETHERLANDS

WEST FRISIAN ISLANDS

WADDENZEE

NORTH SEA

IJSSELMEER

Windmill
Gas
Martini Tower (Groningen)
Groningen
Potatoes
Sugar beet
Cattle
Hunebeds (Prehistoric Monuments)
Cyclists
Hengelo
Enschede
Horses
Beef cattle
Zwolle
IJssel
Apeldoorn
Arnhem
Rhine
Fruit
Nijmegen
Maas (Meuse)
Venlo
Asparagus
Terns
Avocet
Leeuwarden
Ice skating
Wooden clogs
Bulbs
Yachting
Wheat
Canal-side houses
Traditional Dutch costume
Utrecht Cathedral Tower
Waal
's-Hertogenbosch Cathedral
Pigs
Eindhoven
Wheat
Cyclist
Sheep
Cheese porters
Alkmaar
Edam cheese
Haarlem
Amsterdam
Bulbs
Diamond cutting
Leiden
Vegetables
Hilversum
Utrecht
Lek
Rotterdam
Dordrecht
Windmill
Breda
Tilburg
Electronics
Antwerp Cathedral
Antwerp
Port of Antwerp
Herrings
Tourism
THE HAGUE
Delft pottery
Container terminal (Rotterdam)
Scheldt
Plaice
Dam (sea barrier)
Ferry
Ghent
Maison des Franc-Bateliers (Ghent)
Bruges Town Hall
Bruges
Ostend
Shrimps
Tourism
Lace-making

BELGIUM

LUXEMBOURG

LUXEMBOURG

Wine

CLERVAUX

LUXEMBOURG

Esch-sur-Alzette

MT BOTRANGE 694 m

Maastricht

Iron and steel

Wild boar

Liège

Deer

Crystal

Louvain Town Hall

Apples

Beer

Meuse

Namur

BELGIUM

THE ARDENNES FOREST

WALZIN

A R D E N N E S

Charleroi

Chocolates

BRUSSELS

Sambre

Pigs

EC HEADQUARTERS

Mons

Iron and steel

Vegetables

Oudenaarde

Tournai

Beef cattle

Kortrijk

TOURNAI CATHEDRAL

Beer

F R A N C E

AMSTERDAM

Amsterdam, one of the largest cities in the Netherlands, is named after a dam which was built on the River Amstel in the 13th century. Like much of the country, Amsterdam lies below sea level. Large parts of the city are built on huge wooden or concrete piles sunk deep into the soggy ground. A network of canals more than 80 km (50 miles long) criss-crosses the city and helps to drain the land.

By the end of the 16th century, Amsterdam had become the leading port in the Netherlands. For the next hundred years it was also Europe's most important port and trading centre and specialized in trade with the Far East. Many of the famous buildings in the city centre, such as the Royal Palace and the Stock Exchange, date from this period.

Today Amsterdam is a major commercial and financial centre. Many of its industries, such as processing tobacco, coffee, tea and other imported goods, diamond cutting, and shipbuilding, have developed from its historical trading connections.

The Royal Palace   *Nieuwe Kerk*

Dam Square   *The National Monument*

FACTS AND FIGURES

BELGIUM
Capital: Brussels
Area: 30,514 sq km (11,781 sq miles)
Population: 10,000,000
Languages: French, Dutch, some German
Religion: Christian
Currency: Belgian franc

LUXEMBOURG
Capital: Luxembourg
Area: 2,586 sq km (998 sq miles)
Population: 400,000
Languages: Letzeburgesch, French, German
Religion: Christian
Currencies: Luxembourg franc, Belgian franc

THE NETHERLANDS
National capital: Amsterdam
Seat of government: The Hague
Area: 40,844 sq km (15,770 sq miles)
Population: 15,300,000
Language: Dutch
Religion: Christian
Currency: Guilder

Every two years a festival of flowers takes place in the Grande Place in the centre of Brussels in Belgium.

The historic city of Bruges in Belgium is the centre of the country's lace-making industry.

Highest mountain: Mt Botrange (Belgium), 694 m (2,277 ft).
Lowest point: Prins Alexander Polder (Netherlands), 6.7 m (22 ft) below sea level.
Largest metropolitan areas: Brussels (Belgium), 950,400; Amsterdam (Netherlands), 1,091,400; Rotterdam (Netherlands), 1,069,400; The Hague (Netherlands), 694,400.

Rotterdam in the Netherlands is the world's largest port. It has 122 km (76 miles) of quayside.

80 Kilometres
50 Miles

A
B
C
D
E
F
G
H
I
J
K
L
M
N
O

SCANDINAVIA

SCANDINAVIA consists of the four countries of Denmark, Norway, Sweden, and Finland, which are situated in northern Europe, and the island of Iceland, which lies in the North Atlantic Ocean.

The landscape of Scandinavia varies from country to country. Denmark is low lying, and much of the land is used for farming. In contrast, almost all of Norway is mountainous, and the country's coastline is dotted with long, narrow bays called fjords. Finland is a land of forests and lakes, while Sweden has an extremely varied landscape, which includes forest, farmland, mountains

and lakes. The central part of Iceland is a plateau of volcanoes, lava fields and glaciers, so most of the people live around the coast. The people of Scandinavia are the descendants of the Vikings, who lived there about 1,000 years ago. The Vikings are usually remembered as warriors and seafarers, but for most of the time they lived peacefully as farmers and fishermen.

Scandinavia has important natural resources, including the timber in its large forests, fish in the surrounding seas, iron ore in northern Sweden, and oil and natural gas in the North Sea off the coast of Norway. Today, the Scandinavian countries all have successful industrial economies, and their people enjoy a high standard of living.

THE FJORDS

During the last great Ice Age, huge ice sheets and glaciers formed over Scandinavia. The moving ice carved out deep, steep-sided valleys. When the ice sheets began to melt, about 11,000 years ago, many of these valleys were filled by the sea, forming the famous Norwegian fjords.

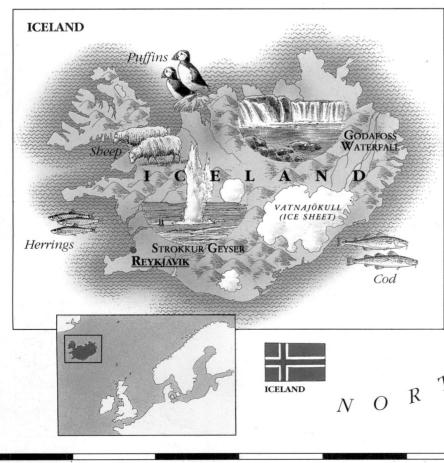

ICELAND

Puffins

Sheep

GODAFOSS
WATERFALL

I C E L A N D

*VATNAJÖKULL
(ICE SHEET)*

Herrings

STROKKUR GEYSER

REYKJAVÍK

Cod

ICELAND

DENMARK

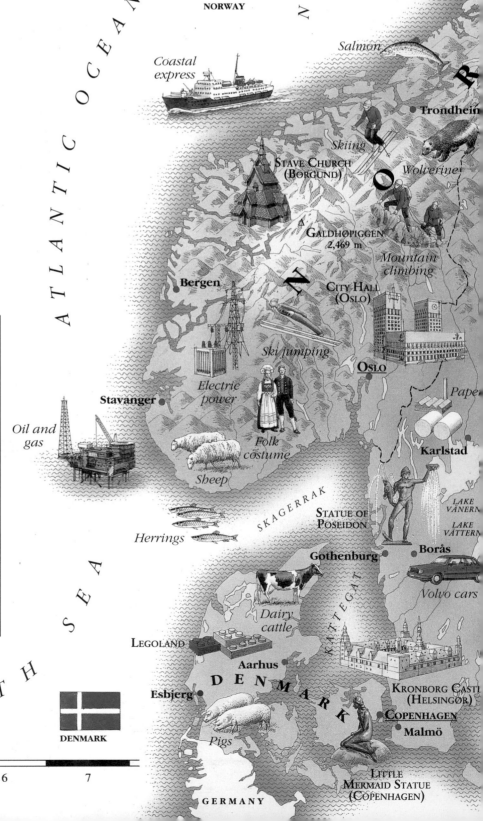

NORWEGIAN SEA

NORWAY

*Fishing
trawler*

Salmon

ATLANTIC OCEAN

*Coastal
express*

Trondheim

Skiing

STAVE CHURCH
(BORGUND)

Wolverine

GALDHØPIGGEN
2,469 m

*Mountain
climbing*

Bergen

CITY HALL
(OSLO)

Ski jumping

OSLO

*Electric
power*

Stavanger

Pape

*Oil and
gas*

*Folk
costume*

Karlstad

Sheep

SKAGERRAK

Statue of
POSEIDON

LAKE
VÄNERN

LAKE
VÄTTERN

Herrings

Gothenburg

Borås

Dairy
cattle

Volvo cars

KATTEGAT

LEGOLAND

DENMARK

Aarhus

KRONBORG CASTLE
(HELSINGØR)

Esbjerg

COPENHAGEN

Malmö

NORTH SEA

Pigs

GERMANY

LITTLE
MERMAID STATUE
(COPENHAGEN)

FACTS AND FIGURES

Scandinavia's large forests are an important source of wealth. Much of the timber is used to make paper.

Highest mountain: Galdhøpiggen (Norway), 2,469 m (8,100 ft).

Largest lake: Lake Vänern (Sweden), 5,580 sq km (2,155 sq miles).

Largest metropolitan areas: Copenhagen (Denmark), 1,342,700; Stockholm (Sweden), 1,450,000; Helsinki (Finland), 1,040,000; Oslo (Norway), 720,000; Gothenborg (Sweden), 710,900.

The city of Copenhagen in Denmark has been an important port and trading centre since the Middle Ages.

DENMARK
Capital: Copenhagen
Area: 43,077 sq km (16,632 sq miles)
Population: 5,200,000
Language: Danish
Religion: Christian
Currency: Danish krone
Government: Monarchy

FINLAND
Capital: Helsinki
Area: 338,127 sq km (130,551 sq miles)
Population: 5,000,000
Languages: Finnish, Swedish, Lappish
Religion: Christian
Currency: Markka
Government: Republic

ICELAND
Capital: Reykjavik
Area: 103,000 sq km (39,768 sq miles)
Population: 300,000
Language: Icelandic
Religion: Christian
Currency: Icelandic krona
Government: Republic

NORWAY
Capital: Oslo
Area: 323,895 sq km (125,056 sq miles)
Population: 4,300,000
Languages: Norwegian, Lappish
Religion: Christian
Currency: Norwegian krone
Government: Monarchy

SWEDEN
Capital: Stockholm
Area: 440,945 sq km (170,250 sq miles)
Population: 8,700,000
Language: Swedish, Lappish
Religion: Christian
Currency: Swedish krona
Government: Monarchy

In central Iceland, volcanoes and hot water springs lie next to frozen rivers of ice, called glaciers.

GERMANY, AUSTRIA, AND SWITZERLAND

THE LANDSCAPE in this region varies greatly, changing from flat plains in the north to high mountains in the south. It is crossed by two of Europe's longest rivers: the Rhine, which flows northwards to the North Sea, and the Danube, which flows eastwards to the Black Sea.

For hundreds of years, the area now called Germany consisted of many small independent states. These states were first united to form a single country in 1871. Germany rapidly became an important industrial and political power. In this century, Germany was defeated in two world wars. After World War II the country was split into two parts: the Federal Republic of Germany (West Germany) and the communist German Democratic Republic (East Germany). This split lasted for over 40 years. During this period relations between the two countries were often hostile because of their different political systems. The two German states were reunited in 1990, following the collapse of the communist government in East Germany. Today, Germany is amongst the world's most successful industrial nations and is the wealthiest country in Europe.

South of Germany lie the mountainous countries of Austria and Switzerland. Tourism, particularly winter sports, is an important source of wealth for both these countries. Switzerland is famous for its watches and scientific instruments, and is also a major banking and business centre. The country has been neutral since 1815 and has stayed out of all the wars that have affected Europe since that time. Austria is also neutral. The tiny country of Liechtenstein, which lies between Switzerland and Austria, is only about 24 km (15 miles) long and 8 km (5 miles) wide.

THE ALPS

EIGER
3,970 m

MÖNCH
4,099 m

JUNGFRAU
4,158 m

The Alps are the longest and highest mountain range in western Europe. They stretch from southeastern France, through Italy, Switzerland, Austria, Slovenia, and Croatia, into Yugoslavia – a distance of about 1,200 km (750 miles). People from around the world visit the Alps to take part in sports such as skiing and mountaineering.

13   14   15   16   17   18   19   20   21   22   23

BALTIC SEA

RÜGEN

Rostock

Storks

Sugar beet

Dairy cattle

Schwerin

Sheep

Shipbuilding

GERMANY

BRANDENBURG GATE

Machinery   **●Berlin**

Potsdam

Magdeburg

Pigs

Poultry

Halle

Leipzig

Iron and steel

Chemnitz

Zwickau

Dresden

Textiles

ZWINGER PALACE

P O L A N D

FACTS AND FIGURES

Belvedere Castle in Vienna was built for the Habsburg family, who ruled Austria for many centuries.

Longest rivers: Danube, 2,858 km (1,776 miles); Rhine, 1,320 km (820 miles).

Largest lakes: Lake Geneva (Switzerland-France), 580 sq km (224 sq miles); Lake Constance (Germany-Switzerland-Austria), 539 sq km (208 sq miles).

Largest cities: Berlin (Germany), 3,446,000; Hamburg (Germany), 1,660,700; Vienna (Austria), 1,539,900; Munich (Germany), 1,236,500; Zurich (Switzerland), 1,158,100. Cologne (Germany), 955,500; Frankfurt (Germany), 647,200; Essen (Germany), 626,100;

World's tallest spire: The cathedral of Ulm in Germany has the world's tallest church spire. It is 161 m (528 ft) high.

Busiest canal: The Kiel Canal in Germany is the busiest in the world. In 1989 over 45,000 ships passed through it on their way between the North Sea and the Baltic Sea.

World's longest road tunnel: St Gotthard tunnel in Switzerland runs under the Alps, and is 16.32 km (10.14 miles) long.

World's biggest roof: The glass roof over the Olympic Stadium in Munich measures 85,000 sq m (914,940 sq ft).

Many dairy cows graze on the slopes of the Alps. Their milk is used to make the famous Swiss chocolate.

AUSTRIA
Capital: Vienna
Area: 83,853 sq km (32,375 sq miles)
Population: 7,800,000
Language: German
Religion: Christian
Currency: Schilling
Government: Republic

GERMANY
Capital: Berlin
Seat of government: Bonn
Area: 356,910 sq km (137,804 sq miles)
Population: 80,600,000
Language: German
Religion: Christian
Currency: Deutsche Mark
Government: Republic

LIECHTENSTEIN
Capital: Vaduz
Area: 160 sq km (62 sq miles)
Population: 29,400
Language: German
Religion: Christian
Currency: Swiss franc
Government: Principality

SWITZERLAND
Capital: Bern
Area: 41,293 sq km (15,943 sq miles)
Population: 6,900,000
Languages: German, French, Italian
Religion: Christian
Currency: Swiss franc
Government: Republic

The city of Munich in southern Germany is famous for its annual beer festival, the Oktoberfest.

C Z E C H   R E P U B L I C

REGENSBURG CATHEDRAL

Regensburg

Beer

Sugar beet

Electronics

Munich

violins

HOHENSALZBURG CASTLE

Salzburg

MOZART'S BIRTHPLACE

A U S T R I A

Edelweiss

Chamois (type of goat)

Mountain climbing

Skiing

Cakes

Lipizzaner horses

Linz

Danube

Dairy cattle

VIENNA OPERA HOUSE

VIENNA

Iron and steel

Great white heron

Graz

MARIA-HILF-KIRCHE (GRAZ)

AUSTRIA

H U N G A R Y

S L O V E N I A

THE RHINE VALLEY

The Rhine is one of the longest rivers in Europe. It flows from Switzerland through Germany and the Netherlands to the North Sea. Boats can sail up the Rhine as far as Basel in Switzerland, and for this reason the river has been an important European trade route for many centuries. Products such as coal, iron ore and petroleum are still transported by barge along the Rhine today.

In western Germany, the Rhine flows through a spectacular, steep-sided valley dotted with ruined castles, some of which are 800 years old. In many places the sides of the valley have been terraced and are used for growing wine grapes.

One of the famous sights of the Rhine Valley is the Lorelei Rock, which is situated west of Wiesbaden. According to legend, a water nymph at the Lorelei sang to passing sailors and lured them to their deaths on the rocks.

A B C D E F G H I J K L M N O

13   14   15   16   17   18   19   20   21   22   23

ITALY

THE EASILY RECOGNIZABLE BOOT SHAPE OF ITALY is a thin, 800-km (500-miles) long peninsula in southern Europe, which stretches south into the Mediterranean Sea. Nearly three-quarters of the country is hilly or mountainous. In the north, the snow-covered Alps form a barrier between Italy and the rest of Europe. Running down the spine of the country are the Apennines, rugged mountains dotted with hill-top villages and small towns that have hardly changed for centuries. The Mediterranean islands of Sicily and Sardinia are also part of Italy.

Modern Italy, with Rome as its capital, only came into existence in 1870. Before then the area had been a patchwork of independent city states. These states can still be seen today in Italy's 20 "regions". Two of the states have remained independent – the Vatican City in Rome and the Republic of San Marino in northeastern Italy.

Italy has been important since Roman times, when it was the centre of the greatest empire Europe had ever seen. The remains of Roman roads and buildings can still be seen all over the country and beyond. In the 14th–16th centuries, Italy was the centre of an important movement in the arts, called the Renaissance. Many beautiful paintings, sculptures, buildings, and poems were produced in Italy during this period. Amongst Italy's most famous Renaissance writers and artists were Michelangelo, Leonardo da Vinci, Raphael, and Dante. Today millions of tourists each year visit Italy's ancient cities and art treasures.

Modern Italy is an important industrial nation, with large steel, chemical, textile, and car manufacturing industries. However, many Italians still make their living from farming. The main crops are wheat, corn, rice, grapes, and olives, and there are many fishing ports around Italy's coast.

FACTS AND FIGURES

Cars, motorbikes, tractors and trucks are among Italy's most valuable exports. Major manufactures include Fiat, Ferrari, and Lamborghini.

The city of Venice is built on about 120 islands and has canals in place of streets.

Highest mountains: Mont Blanc (Italy-France), 4,807 m (15,770 ft); Monte Rosa (Italy-Switzerland), 4,634 m (15,203 ft).

Longest river: Po, 672 km (418 miles).

Largest lakes: Lake Garda, 370 sq km (143 sq miles); Lake Maggiore, 212 sq km (82 sq miles); Lake Como, 145 sq km (55 sq miles).

Largest metropolitan areas: Milan, 3,750,000; Rome, 3,175,000; Naples, 2,875,000; Turin, 1,550,000.

A horse race called the Palio takes place in Siena each year. The riders wear traditional costumes dating from the 15th century.

ITALY
Capital: Rome
Area: 301,268 sq km (116,320 sq miles)
Population: 57,800,000
Language: Italian
Religion: Christian
Currency: Lira
Government: Republic

MALTA
Capital: Valletta
Area: 316 sq km (122 sq miles)
Population: 400,000
Languages: Maltese, English
Religion: Christian
Currency: Maltese Lira
Government: Republic

SAN MARINO
Capital: San Marino
Area: 61 sq km (23 sq miles)
Population: 23,000
Language: Italian
Religion: Christian
Currency: Italian lira
Government: Republic

VATICAN CITY
Area: 0.44 sq km (0.17 sq miles)
Population: 1,000

Map labels:

AUSTRIA
SLOVENIA
CROATIA
SWITZERLAND
FRANCE

ALPS
APENNINES
LIGURIAN SEA

MONTE ROSA 4,634 m
MONT BLANC 4,807 m
PINNACLES OF THE DOLOMITES

Chamois (type of goat)
Ibex (type of goat)
Marmots
Skiing
Wine
Trieste
Udine
Bolzano
Trento
Venice
St Mark's Square
Padua
Verona
Adige
Mantua
Ferrara
Po
Bologna
Ravenna
Rimini
SAN MARINO
Old Town of San Marino
Sole
Ancona
Venetian gondolier
Cruise liner
Tourism
Santa Chiara (Assisi)
Assisi
Perugia
Florence Cathedral
Florence
Siena
The Palio
Leaning Tower of Pisa
Pisa
Arno
Livorno
Elba
Squid
La Spezia
Tourism
Shellfish
Genoa
Tourism
Parmesan cheese
Rice
Milan Cathedral
Milan
Monza
Como
Bergamo
LAKE COMO
LAKE MAGGIORE
Brescia
Violins
LAKE GARDA
Cremona
Po
Parma
Modena
Marble quarry
Ferrari cars
Turin
Fiat cars
Wine
Olive trees
Sardines
Ferry boat
Tourism

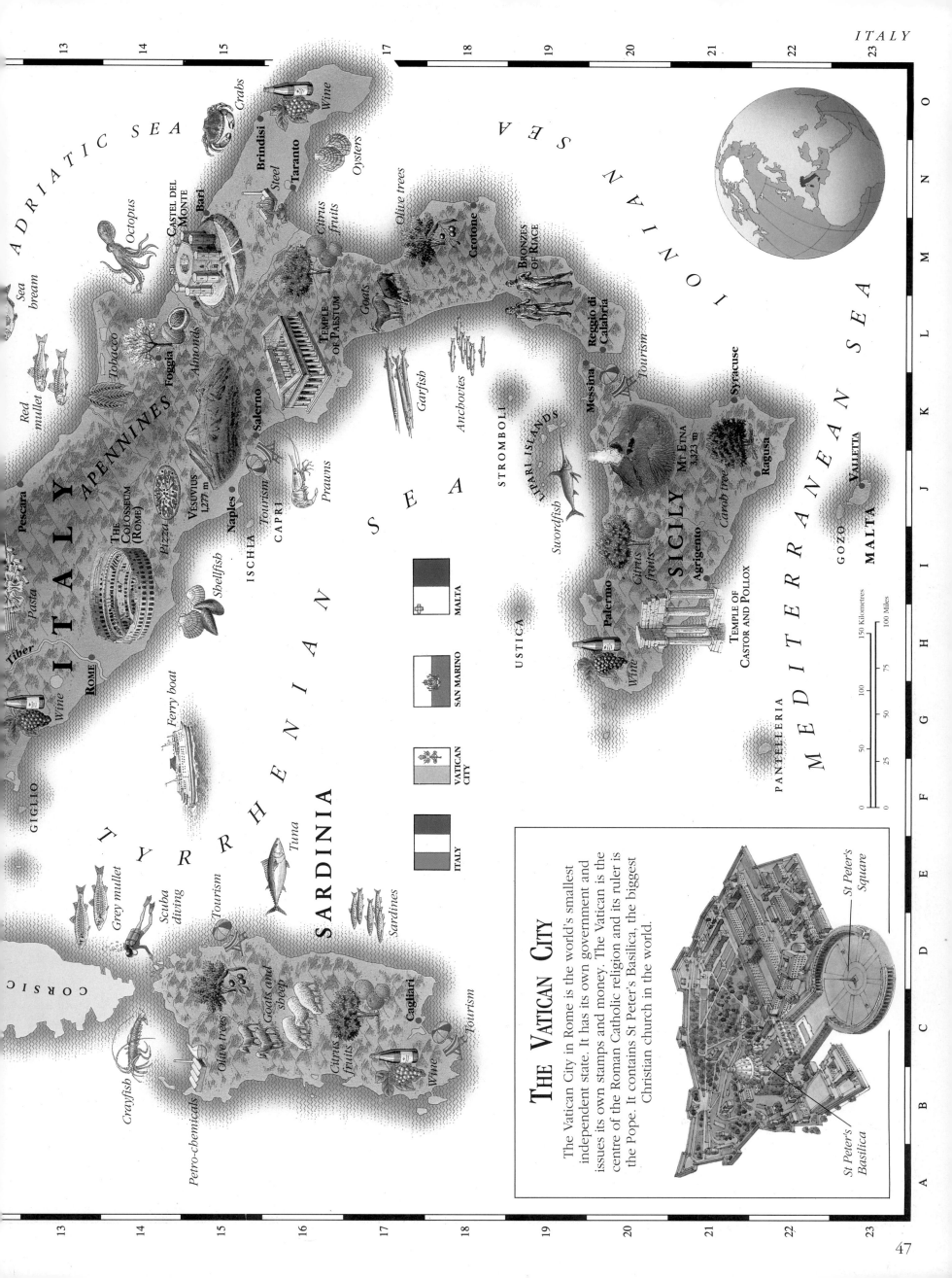

ADRIATIC SEA

Crabs

Wine

Brindisi

Taranto

Steel

Bari

Oysters

CASTEL DEL MONTE

Octopus

Citrus fruits

Olive trees

Sea bream

Goats

Crotone

BRONZES OF RACE

Red mullet

Tobacco

Almonds

Foggia

TEMPLE OF PAESTUM

Reggio di Calabria

IONIAN SEA

Tourism

Garfish

Anchovies

Messina

Tourism

APENNINES

Pescara

Pasta

THE COLOSSEUM (ROME)

VESUVIUS 1,277 m

Salerno

Naples

Tourism

Prawns

ISCHIA

CAPRI

STROMBOLI

LIPARI ISLANDS

Swordfish

Mt ETNA 3,323 m

Syracuse

SICILY

Carob tree

Ragusa

Pizza

ITALY

Shellfish

TYRRHENIAN SEA

USTICA

Palermo

Agrigento

Citrus fruits

VALLETTA

GOZO

MALTA

Tiber

ROME

Wine

Ferry boat

MALTA

SAN MARINO

VATICAN CITY

Wine

TEMPLE OF CASTOR AND POLLOX

MEDITERRANEAN SEA

GIGLIO

ITALY

PANTELLERIA

CORSIC

Grey mullet

Scuba diving

Tourism

Tuna

SARDINIA

Sardines

Petro-chemicals

Olive trees

Goats and sheep

Citrus fruits

Cagliari

Tourism

Crayfish

Wine

Tourism

THE VATICAN CITY

The Vatican City in Rome is the world's smallest independent state. It has its own government and issues its own stamps and money. The Vatican is the centre of the Roman Catholic religion and its ruler is the Pope. It contains St Peter's Basilica, the biggest Christian church in the world.

St Peter's Square

St Peter's Basilica

150 Kilometres

100 Miles

47

SPAIN AND PORTUGAL

THE COUNTRIES of Spain and Portugal occupy a large, square block of land called the Iberian Peninsula in the southwest of Europe. The peninsula also contains the tiny independent state of Andorra and the British colony of Gibraltar. Over the centuries, Spain and Portugal have been invaded and settled by many different peoples, including the Romans and the Moors – an Arab people from North Africa who ruled much of Spain for nearly eight centuries.

Both Spain and Portugal have a long history of exploring and trading by sea. Christopher Columbus set out from Spain when he sailed to America in 1492. In 1497 the Portuguese explorer, Vasco da Gama, became the first person to sail around Africa to India. Settlers followed the explorers, and during the 16th century Spain and Portugal came to rule vast empires in North and South America, Asia, and Africa.

Today, many people in Spain and Portugal make their living from farming or fishing. Both countries also have important manufacturing industries, producing steel, ships, cars, chemicals, and textiles. Tourism is a major source of wealth in both countries.

PORTUGAL

THE WINE TRADE

Spain and Portugal are famous for their "fortified" wines, such as sherry and port. These contain more alcohol than normal wine because brandy is added to the grape juice to fortify, or strengthen, it. This was originally done to stop the wine going off while it was shipped abroad. Fortified wines are left in wooden casks to mature for at least three years. Both sherry and port are named after the towns where they are produced – sherry comes from Jerez de la Frontera in southern Spain, and port from Porto in northern Portugal.

BAY OF BISC

Shellfish

Fish packing

Iron and steel

Gijón

Santan

Oviedo

Apples

Coal

CAVE PAINTING (ALTAMIRA)

La Coruña

Horses

Brown bear

CATHEDRAL OF SANTIAGO DE COMPOSTELA

Santiago

Potatoes

León

LEÓN CATHEDRAL

Cattle

Wheat

Vigo

Minho

Fish packing

Egyptian vulture

Textiles

Braga

COCKEREL OF BARCELOS

Valladolid

Anchovies

Porto

Douro

Cattle

S P

Port wine

Salamanca

HOUSE OF SHELLS (SALAMANCA)

Segovia

Transporting port wine

Potatoes

Ávila

Mackerel

Fish packing

Rugs

Tole

Coimbra

STATUE OF PIZARRO (TRUJILLO)

Pilchards

PORTUGAL

Tagus

Toledo

TOLEDO CATHEDRAL

BELÉM TOWER

Olive trees

Wine

ROMAN THEATRE

Tagus

ROMAN TEMPLE (ÉVORA)

Mérida

Guadiana

Manchego cheese

LISBON

Badajoz

Sheep

Setúbal

Windmill

Fish packing

Bulls

CÓRDOBA MOSQUE

Sardines

Cork oak

SEVILLE CATHEDRAL

Córdoba

Guadalquivir

Citrus fruits

Pardel lynx

Seville

Holy week procession (Seville)

Tourism

Guadiana

Tourism

Faro

Sherry

Wine

Málaga

Lobster

Jerez de la Frontera

Cádiz

ROCK OF GIBRALTAR

GIBRALTAR

STRAIT OF GIBRALTAR

M

Ceuta (Spain)

Tuna

ATLANTIC OCEAN

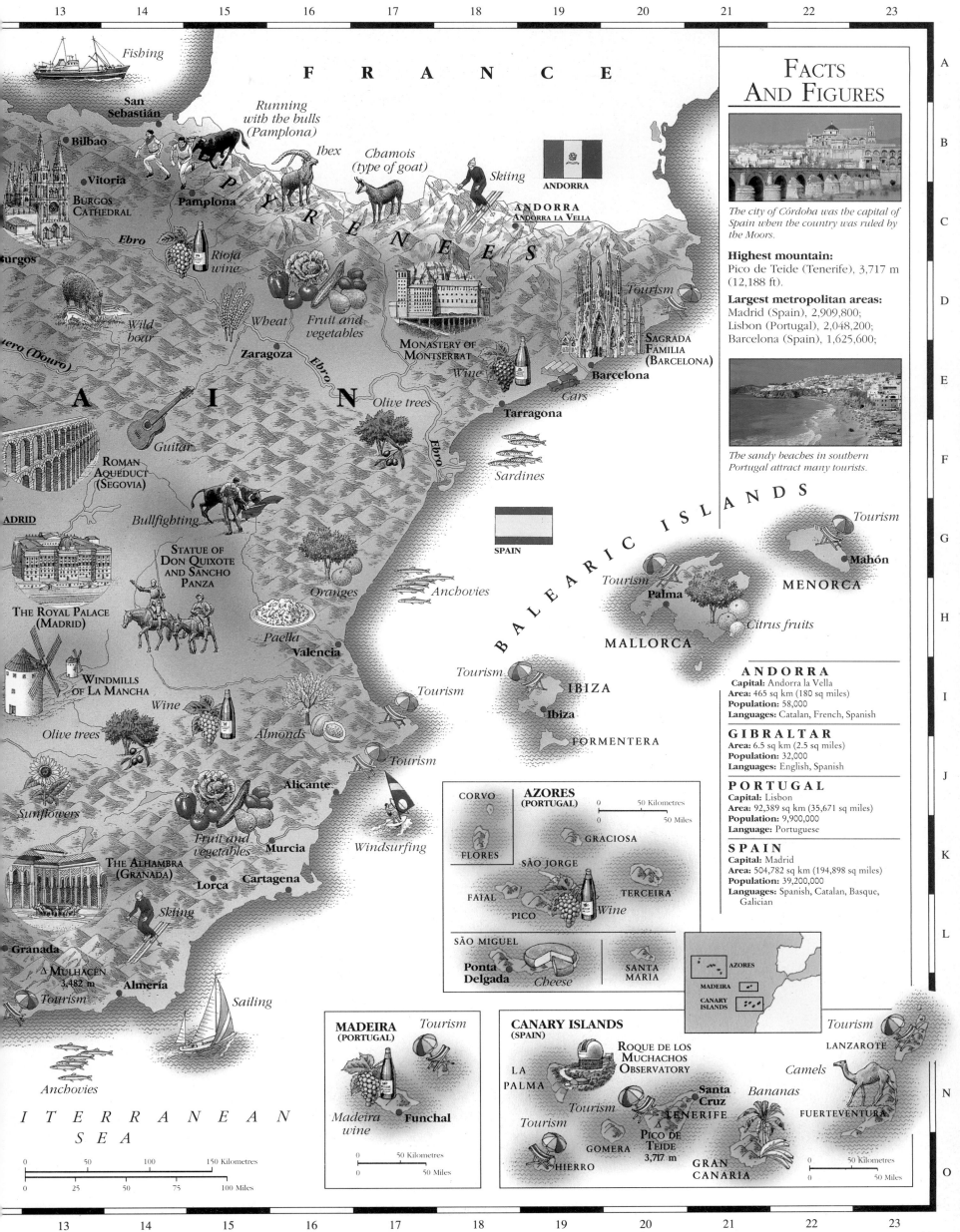

FACTS AND FIGURES

The city of Córdoba was the capital of Spain when the country was ruled by the Moors.

Highest mountain:
Pico de Teide (Tenerife), 3,717 m (12,188 ft).

Largest metropolitan areas:
Madrid (Spain), 2,909,800;
Lisbon (Portugal), 2,048,200;
Barcelona (Spain), 1,625,600;

The sandy beaches in southern Portugal attract many tourists.

ANDORRA
Capital: Andorra la Vella
Area: 465 sq km (180 sq miles)
Population: 58,000
Languages: Catalan, French, Spanish

GIBRALTAR
Area: 6.5 sq km (2.5 sq miles)
Population: 32,000
Languages: English, Spanish

PORTUGAL
Capital: Lisbon
Area: 92,389 sq km (35,671 sq miles)
Population: 9,900,000
Language: Portuguese

SPAIN
Capital: Madrid
Area: 504,782 sq km (194,898 sq miles)
Population: 39,200,000
Languages: Spanish, Catalan, Basque, Galician

CENTRAL AND EASTERN EUROPE

THIS REGION has always been one of the most unstable parts of Europe, and the boundaries between the countries have changed many times. After World War II, all the countries in this region, apart from Greece, became part of the "Eastern Bloc". They had communist governments and strong links with the former USSR. In recent years there have been important political changes in the region. Many of the countries are now establishing democratic forms of government and are building closer links with their neighbours in Western Europe.

The northern part of this region is dominated by Poland. The country of Poland has been much fought over, and for long periods it did not exist as a separate nation. Poland is rich in coal and copper, and has large textile, iron, steel, and shipbuilding industries. Farming is also important: the main crops are potatoes, wheat, and sugar beet. South of Poland lie the Czech Republic and Slovakia. This area was formerly one country, called Czechoslovakia. It was inhabited by two separate peoples – the Czechs and the Slovaks – who spoke different languages. In 1993 Czechoslovakia split apart to form the two countries there today.

To the south lies the area known as the Balkans, which includes the countries of Greece, Albania, Bosnia and Herzegovina, Croatia, Slovenia, Macedonia, Yugoslavia, Bulgaria, Romania, and Hungary. Many of the countries in the Balkans were only formed during the rearrangement of European borders at the end of the two World Wars. More recently, the republics of Bosnia and Hercegovina, Croatia, Macedonia, and Slovenia broke away from Yugoslavia and were recognized as independent countries.

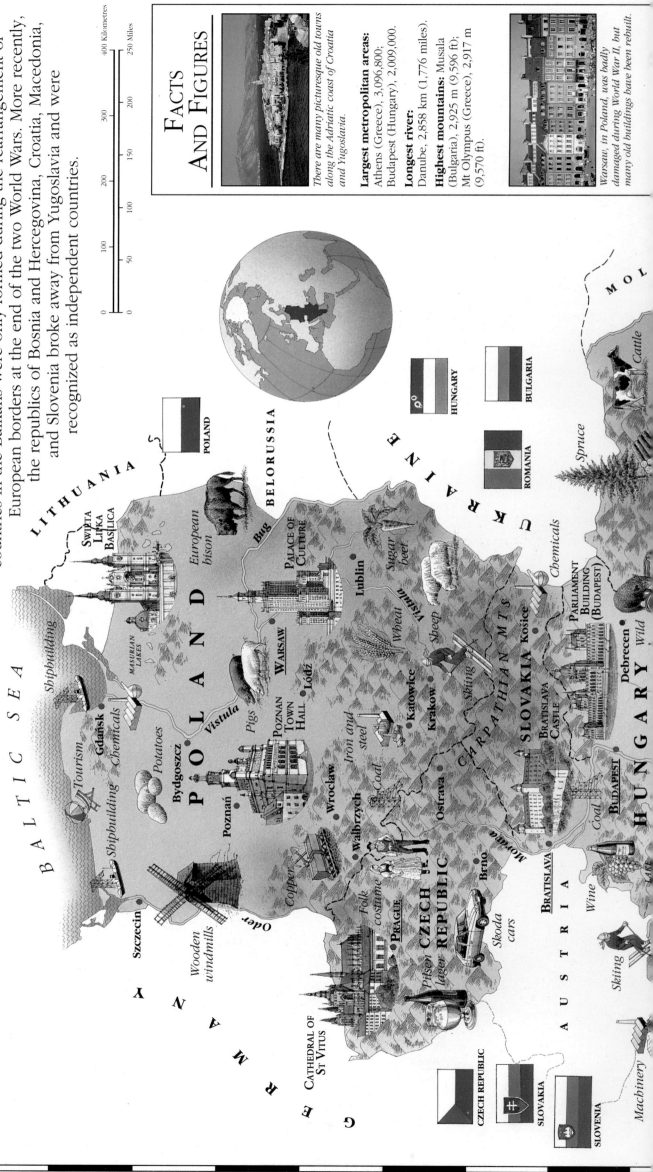

FACTS AND FIGURES

There are many picturesque old towns along the Adriatic coast of Croatia and Yugoslavia.

Largest metropolitan areas:
Athens (Greece), 3,096,800;
Budapest (Hungary), 2,009,000.

Longest river:
Danube, 2,858 km (1,776 miles).

Highest mountains: Musala (Bulgaria), 2,925 m (9,596 ft); Mt Olympus (Greece), 2,917 m (9,570 ft).

Warsaw, in Poland, was badly damaged during World War II, but many old buildings have been rebuilt.

400 Kilometres
250 Miles

300
200
150
100
50
0

200
100
0

POLAND

HUNGARY

BULGARIA

ROMANIA

CZECH REPUBLIC

SLOVAKIA

SLOVENIA

LITHUANIA

BELORUSSIA

UKRAINE

MOL

BALTIC SEA

Shipbuilding

Tourism

Gdańsk

Chemicals

Szczecin

Wooden windmills

Shipbuilding

Potatoes

Oder

ŚWIĘTA LIPKA BASILICA

MASURIAN LAKES

European bison

Bug

PALACE OF CULTURE

Lublin

Sugar beet

Chemicals

Vistula

WARSAW

Bydgoszcz

POLAND

Pigs

Wheat

Sheep

POZNAN TOWN HALL

Poznań

Vistula

Wrocław

Iron and steel

Wałbrzych

Coal

Katowice

Kraków

Ostrava

CARPATHIAN MTS

Skiing

Košice

SLOVAKIA

BRATISLAVA CASTLE

PARLIAMENT BUILDING (BUDAPEST)

Debrecen

Copper

CATHEDRAL OF ST VITUS

Folk costume

PRAGUE

CZECH REPUBLIC

Pilsen lager

Skoda cars

Brno

Moravia

BRATISLAVA

Wine

BUDAPEST

HUNGARY

Wild

Coal

Skiing

AUSTRIA

Skiing

Machinery

GERMANY

Cattle

Spruce

Chemicals

ALBANIA
Capital: Tirana
Area: 28,748 sq km (11,099 sq miles)
Population: 3,300,000

BOSNIA & HERZEGOVINA
Capital: Sarajevo
Area: 51,129 sq km (19,741 sq miles)
Population: 4,500,000

BULGARIA
Capital: Sofia
Area: 110,912 sq km (42,823 sq miles)
Population: 8,900,000

CROATIA
Capital: Zagreb
Area: 56,538 sq km (21,829 sq miles)
Population: 4,900,000

CZECH REPUBLIC
Capital: Prague
Area: 78,864 sq km (30,449 sq miles)
Population: 10,400,000

GREECE
Capital: Athens
Area: 131,990 sq km (50,961 sq miles)
Population: 10,200,000

HUNGARY
Capital: Budapest
Area: 93,032 sq km (35,919 sq miles)
Population: 10,500,000

MACEDONIA
Capital: Skopje
Area: 25,713 sq km (9,928 sq miles)
Population: 1,900,000

POLAND
Capital: Warsaw
Area: 312,685 sq km (120,728 sq miles)
Population: 38,500,000

ROMANIA
Capital: Bucharest
Area: 237,500 sq km (91,699 sq miles)
Population: 23,400,000

SLOVAKIA
Capital: Bratislava
Area: 49,035 sq km (18,932 sq miles)
Population: 5,300,000

SLOVENIA
Capital: Ljubljana
Area: 20,251 sq km (7,819 sq miles)
Population: 2,000,000

YUGOSLAVIA
Capital: Belgrade
Area: 102,173 sq km (39,449 sq miles)
Population: 10,600,000

The Parliament Building, Budapest.

THE ACROPOLIS

The Acropolis is a rocky hill in the centre of Athens in Greece. On the Acropolis are the remains of magnificent temples built by the Ancient Greeks in the 5th century BC. The largest and most famous of these temples is the Parthenon. It originally contained a huge statue of the goddess Athene, 12 m (39 ft) high, which was covered in gold and ivory. The entrance to the Acropolis was through a magnificent gateway called the Propylaea.

51

ASIA

Guilin, China.

ASIA is the largest continent in the world, occupying nearly a third of the world's total land area. It contains the world's highest point (Mount Everest), as well as its lowest (the Dead Sea). Asia also has the largest population of any continent – six out of every ten people in the world live there. All the world's major religions – including Judaism, Islam, Buddhism, Christianity, Confucianism, and Hinduism – originated in Asia.

In a continent of this size, stretching from the Arctic to the Equator, there are great contrasts. The climate ranges from some of the coldest places on Earth to some of the hottest, and from some of the driest places to some of the wettest. Asia contains the world's largest country (the Russian Federation) and some of its smallest countries. In parts of Asia there are huge concentrations of people, yet there are also vast regions which are almost uninhabited.

Siberia, the Asian part of the Russian Federation, is mainly covered by coniferous forest. It is bitterly cold in winter, and few people live there. Bordering the Russian Federation in the east is China. Most of China's one billion people live in the eastern part of the

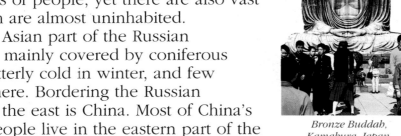

Bronze Buddah, Kamakura, Japan.

country where the land is good for farming. The population of the Gobi Desert and the high plateau of Tibet is very small. South of the Himalayas, the world's highest mountain range, lies Southern Asia, which is often called the Indian subcontinent. Around one billion people live there, mainly along the fertile coasts and on the plains of the Ganges and Indus rivers in the north.

Southwestern Asia is also known as the Middle East. The world's earliest-known civilizations grew up here in the area called the Fertile Crescent, which extends from the Mediterranean Sea across Syria to the land between the Tigris and Euphrates rivers. Among the ancient peoples of the Fertile Crescent were the Sumerians, Assyrians, Babylonians, and Hebrews. This area contrasts sharply with the almost empty deserts of the Arabian Peninsula, occupied by the oil-rich nations of the Persian Gulf.

Southeastern Asia is situated along the Equator. Much of the region is made up of thousands of islands. These include the countries of Indonesia, Malaysia, and the Philippines.

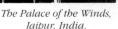

The Palace of the Winds, Jaipur, India.

FACTS ABOUT ASIA

Area: 43,608,000 sq km (16,838,365 sq miles).

Population: 3,422,333,000.

Number of independent countries: 49 (this includes 97 per cent of Turkey, and 72 per cent of the Russian Federation).

Largest countries: The Asian part of the Russian Federation, 12,650,000 sq km (4,884,200 sq miles) – this is only 72 per cent of the total area of the Russian Federation; China, 9,597,000 sq km (3,705,691 sq miles).

Most populated countries: China, 1,205,200,000 (the largest population in the world); India, 896,600,000.

Largest cities: Shanghai (China), 13,510,000; Seoul (South Korea), 10,627,800. Tokyo (Japan), 7,976,000.

Highest mountains: Mt Everest (Nepal-China), the highest in the world, 8,848 m (29,028 ft); K2 (Mt Godwin Austen) (Pakistan-China), 8,611 m (28,250 ft).

Longest rivers: Yangtze (Chang Jiang), 6,300 km (3,915 miles); Yellow River (Huang He), 5,463 km (3,395 miles); Ob-Irtysh, 5,410 km (3,362 miles); Amur, 4,443 km (2,761 miles).

Main deserts: Gobi (Mongolia-China), about 1,295,000 sq km (500,000 sq miles); Thar (Pakistan-India), about 192,000 sq km (74,000 sq miles).

Largest lakes: Caspian Sea, the largest in the world, 371,000 sq km (143,205 sq miles); Aral Sea (Kazakhstan-Uzbekistan), 38,500 sq km (14,865 sq miles).

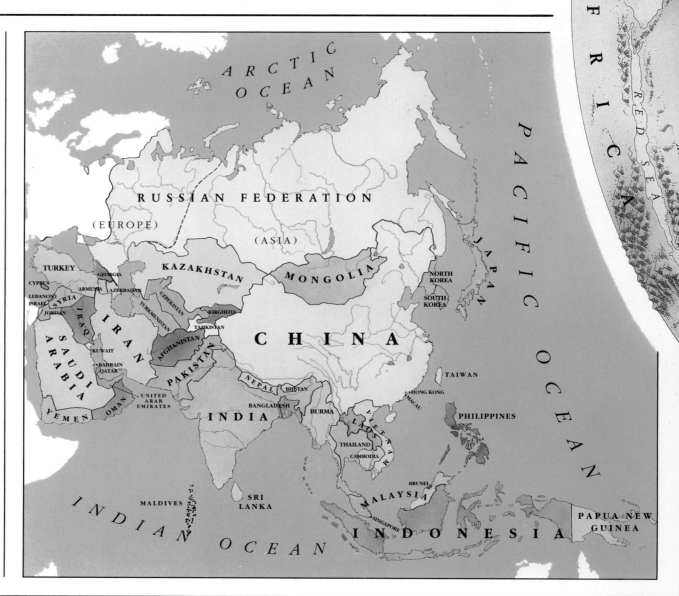

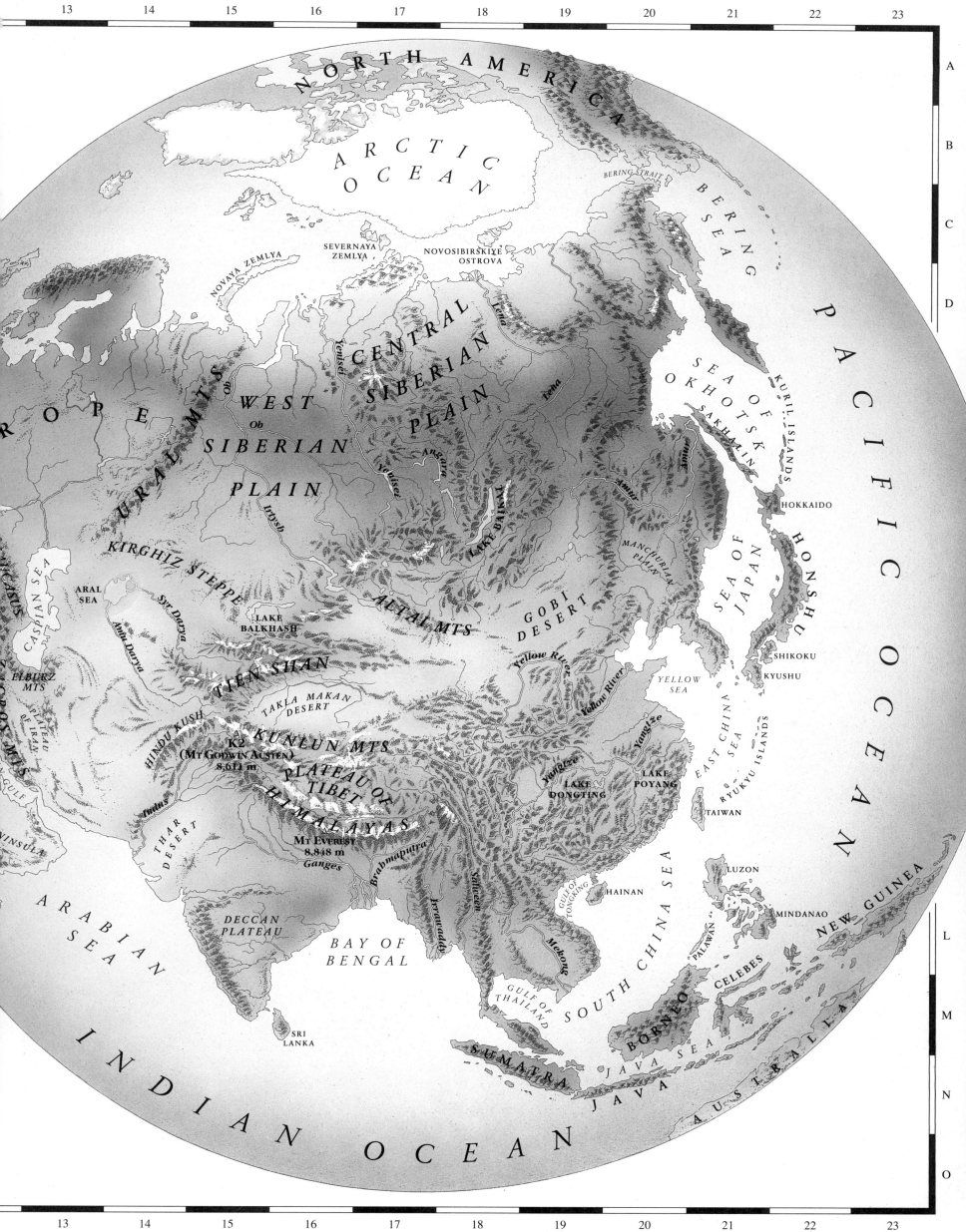

13 14 15 16 17 18 19 20 21 22 23

NORTH AMERICA

ARCTIC OCEAN

BERING SEA

PACIFIC OCEAN

NOVAYA ZEMLYA

SEVERNAYA ZEMLYA

NOVOSIBIRSKIYE OSTROVA

BERING STRAIT

Lena

SEA OF OKHOTSK

KURIL ISLANDS

SAKHALIN

CENTRAL SIBERIAN PLAIN

Yenisei

Ob

WEST SIBERIAN PLAIN

Ob

URAL MTS

Irtysh

KIRGHIZ STEPPE

Angara

LAKE BAIKAL

Lena

Amur

HOKKAIDO

MANCHURIA PLAIN

Amur

SEA OF JAPAN

HONSHU

ARAL SEA

CASPIAN SEA

CAUCASUS MTS

Syr Darya

LAKE BALKHASH

ALTAI MTS

GOBI DESERT

Yellow River

YELLOW SEA

SHIKOKU

KYUSHU

Amu Darya

TIEN SHAN

EAST CHINA SEA

ELBURZ MTS

ZAGROS MTS

PLATEAU OF IRAN

HINDU KUSH

TAKLA MAKAN DESERT

K2 (Mt Godwin Austen) 8,611 m

KUNLUN MTS

PLATEAU OF TIBET

HIMALAYAS

Yellow River

Yangtze

Yangtze

LAKE DONGTING

LAKE POYANG

RYUKYU ISLANDS

TAIWAN

Indus

THAR DESERT

Mt Everest 8,848 m

Ganges

Brahmaputra

Salween

Irrawaddy

Mekong

GULF OF TONGKING

HAINAN

LUZON

SOUTH CHINA SEA

PALAWAN

MINDANAO

NEW GUINEA

GULF

ARABIAN SEA

PENINSULA

DECCAN PLATEAU

BAY OF BENGAL

GULF OF THAILAND

BORNEO

CELEBES

AUSTRALIA

SRI LANKA

SUMATRA

JAVA SEA

JAVA

INDIAN OCEAN

EUROPE

A B C D L M N O

13 14 15 16 17 18 19 20 21 22 23

Northern Eurasia

THIS REGION SPANS TWO CONTINENTS, Europe in the west and Asia in the east. They are separated by the Ural Mountains. The Asian part is much bigger, occupying about 75 per cent of the land area, but only about 35 per cent of the people live there. To the east lies Siberia, much of which is covered by a huge uninhabited wilderness of coniferous trees. The climate there is extremely cold, and in winter the temperature in the north regularly falls below -45°C (-49°F), but this area is rich in precious stones and oil.

From 1922 to 1991, northern Eurasia was one vast country, called the Union of Soviet Socialist Republics, or USSR. It was the world's largest country and was made up of 15 republics, all with communist governments. In 1991, the USSR split apart and all the republics became independent countries. The largest of them – the Russian Federation – remained dominant and succeeded in drawing many of the new nations together in a Commonwealth of Independent States.

GERMANY
BALTIC SEA
FINLAND
CZECH REPUBLIC
Traditional Latvian costume
Tourism
Tourism
TALLINN
ESTONIA
Kaliningrad
RUSSIAN FEDERATION
RIGA
LATVIA
LITHUANIA
Amber jewellery
LITHUANIA
Kaunas
LATVIA
ESTONIA
Pine trees
Traditional Estonian costume
POLAND
Sugar beet
Neman
VILNIUS
Flax
SLOVAKIA
Traditional Ukrainian costume
Cars and tractors
Wheat
MINSK
RUSSIAN FEDERATION
HUNGARY
Lvov
Potatoes
BELORUSSIA
Pripet
Pigs
Traditional Belorussian costume
CATHEDRAL OF ST GEORGE, LVOV
Dniester
Corn
Beef cattle
CHURCH OF ST ANDREW, KIEV
Gomel
BELORUSSIA
ROMANIA
Cattle
Prunes
KIEV
Pigs
Traditional Moldavian costume
MOLDAVIA
KISHINEV
UKRAINE
Wheat
Cars
MOLDAVIA
Odessa
Coal
Dnieper
Sugar beet
KHARKOV
Nikolayev
Iron ore
Dnepropetrovsk
UKRAINE
Warship
Sunflowers
Iron and steel
Wheat
Caviar
Donetsk
RUSSIAN FEDERATION
Tourism
Coal
BLACK SEA
Sturgeon
Iron and steel
Grapes

BALTIC SEA
SWEDEN
WINTER PALACE
RUSSIAN FED.
FINLAND
POLAND
LITHUANIA
LATVIA
St Petersburg
ST BASIL'S CATHEDRAL
BELORUSSIA
MOSCOW
Bolshoi Ballet
UKRAINE
MOLDAVIA
Niznhiy Novgorod
Kirov
Kazan
BLACK SEA
Fur hat
Volga
Samara
Rostov-na-Donu
Volgograd
Cars
Ufa
Grapes
Melons
Astrakhan
Chess
GEORGIA
Caviar
Oil
TBILISI
ARMENIA
Sturgeon
YEREVAN
AZERBAIJAN
Cotton
BAKU
Camels
Oil
ARAL SEA
BAIKONUR SPACE CENTRE
CASPIAN SEA
Cotton
TURKMENISTAN
UZBEKISTAN
IRAN
ASHKHABAD
TASHKENT
GEORGIA
Gas
Carpets
Samarkand
ARMENIA
GUR-EMIR MAUSOLEUM
DUSHANBE
AZERBAIJAN
AFGHANISTAN
PAKISTAN

0   100   200   300 Kilometres
0   50   100   150   200 Miles

FACTS AND FIGURES

The Cathedral of the Annunciation, the Kremlin, Moscow.

Largest lake: Caspian Sea (the largest lake in the world) covers an area of 3,600,000 sq km (143,205 sq miles).

World's longest railway: Trans-Siberian, Moscow to Nakhodka near Vladivostok, 9,438 km (5,864 miles).

ARMENIA
Capital: Yerevan
Area: 29,800 sq km (11,490 sq miles)
Population: 3,376,000
Languages: Armenian, Russian

AZERBAIJAN
Capital: Baku
Area: 86,600 sq km (33,340 sq miles)
Population: 7,300,000
Language: Azerbaijani

BELORUSSIA
Capital: Minsk
Area: 207,600 sq km (80,134 sq miles)
Population: 10,300,000
Languages: Belorussian, Russian

ESTONIA
Capital: Tallinn
Area: 45,100 sq km (17,413 sq miles)
Population: 1,600,000
Language: Estonian

GEORGIA
Capital: Tbilisi
Area: 69,700 sq km (26,900 sq miles)
Population: 5,500,000
Language: Georgian

KAZAKHSTAN
Capital: Alma-Ata
Area: 2,717,300 sq km (1,049,155 sq miles)
Population: 17,200,000
Languages: Kazakh, Russian

KIRGHIZIA
Capital: Bishkek
Area: 198,500 sq km (76,640 sq miles)
Population: 4,600,000
Languages: Kyrgyz, Russian

LATVIA
Capital: Riga
Area: 63,700 sq km (24,595 sq miles)
Population: 2,700,000
Languages: Latvian, Russian

LITHUANIA
Capital: Vilnius
Area: 65,200 sq km (25,170 sq miles)
Population: 3,800,000
Language: Lithuanian

MOLDAVIA
Capital: Kishinev
Area: 33,700 sq km (13,000 sq miles)
Population: 4,400,000
Language: Romanian

RUSSIAN FEDERATION
Capital: Moscow
Area: 17,075,000 sq km (6,592,637 sq miles)
Population: 149,200,000
Language: Russian

TAJIKISTAN
Capital: Dushanbe
Area: 143,100 sq km (55,240 sq miles)
Population: 5,700,000
Languages: Tajik, Russian

TURKMENISTAN
Capital: Ashkhabad
Area: 488,100 sq km (188,455 sq miles)
Population: 4,000,000
Languages: Turkmen, Russian

UKRAINE
Capital: Kiev
Area: 603,700 sq km (231,990 sq miles)
Population: 52,200,000
Languages: Ukrainian, Russian

UZBEKISTAN
Capital: Tashkent
Area: 447,400 sq km (172,741 sq miles)
Population: 21,900,000
Languages: Uzbek, Russian

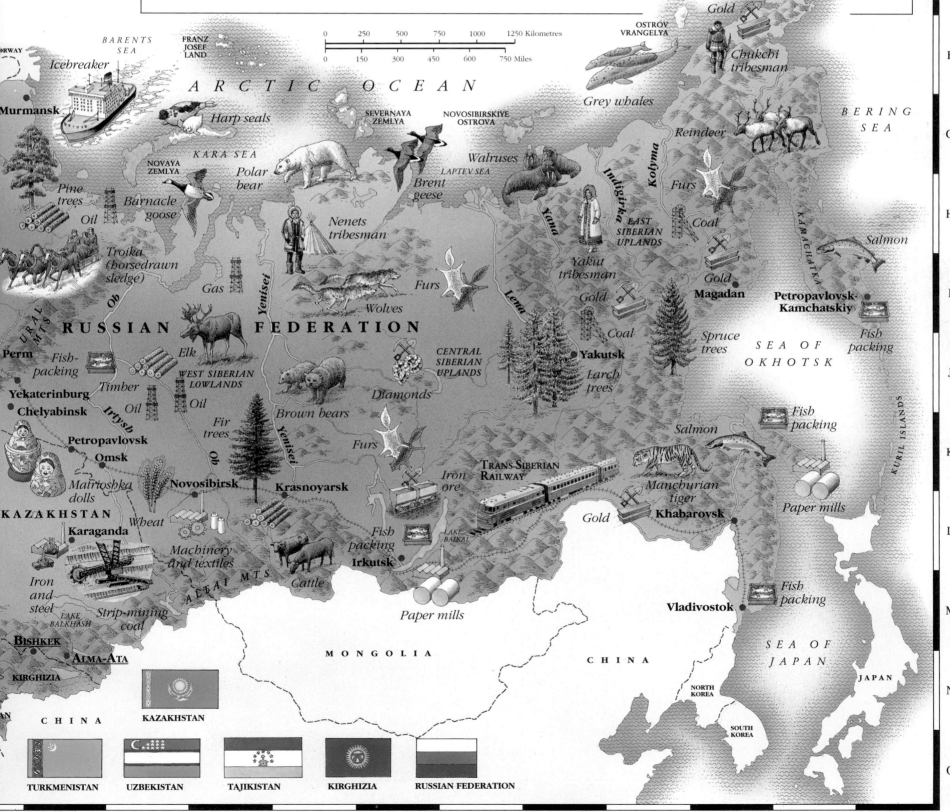

SOUTHWESTERN ASIA

SOUTHWEST ASIA, also known as the Middle East, lies at the join of three continents – Asia, Africa, and Europe. It contains many varied landscapes and cultures. The countries surrounding the Mediterranean are wetter than the others, and crops such as citrus fruits, olives, and wheat are grown here. To the south stretch the huge deserts of Saudi Arabia. Earlier this century, the world's largest deposits of oil were discovered in the countries around the Persian Gulf. The oil-fields in the region now supply the world.

Some of the world's first settled farming communities and towns, grew up in the rich farmlands of the Fertile Crescent, which stretches from the Mediterranean to the area between the Tigris and Euphrates rivers. In recent years, Southwest Asia has been an unsettled region, troubled by a revolution in Iran and a long and bitter war between Iran and Iraq. Civil war in Lebanon has claimed many lives, and there have also been wars between Israel and its Arab neighbours.

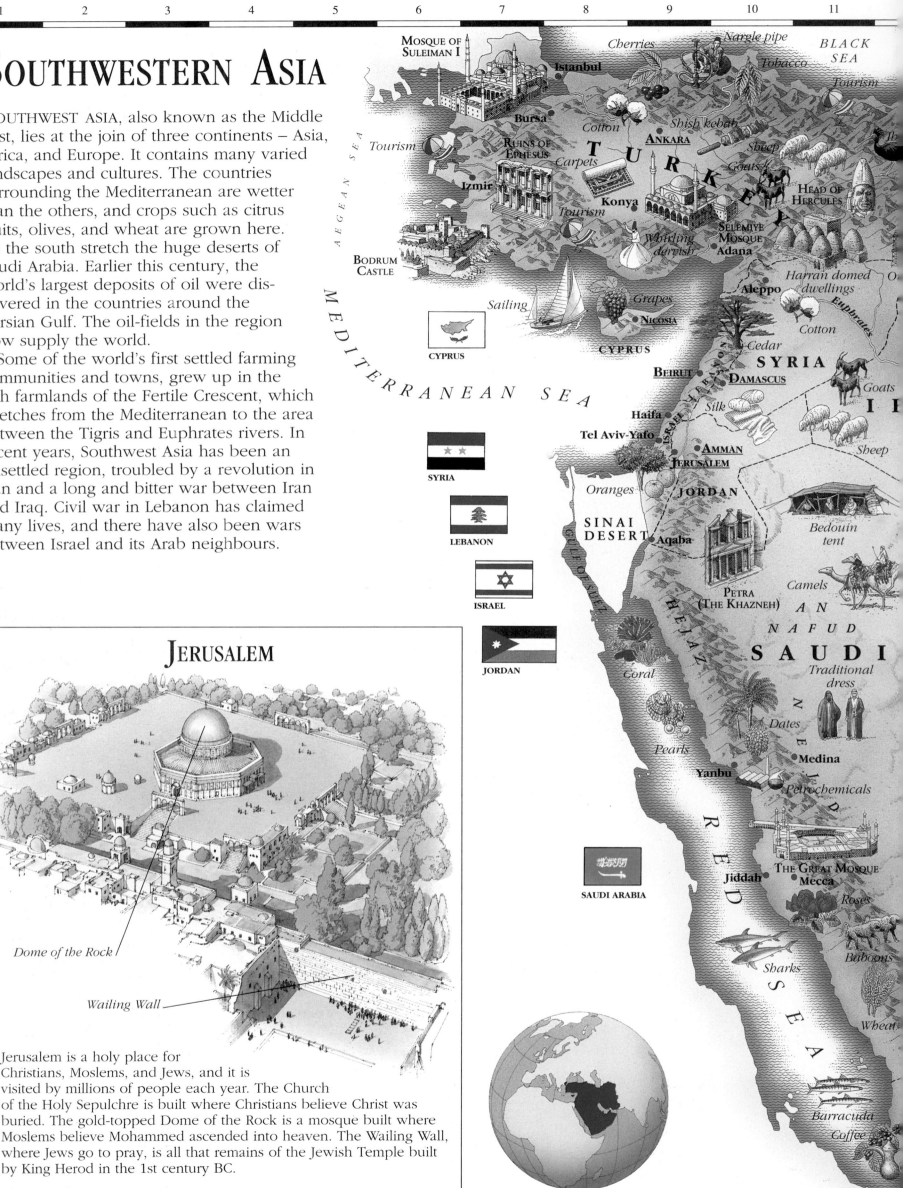

MEDITERRANEAN SEA

AEGEAN SEA

Mosque of Suleiman I

Istanbul

Bursa

Ruins of Ephesus

Izmir

Bodrum Castle

Tourism

Sailing

CYPRUS

Cherries

Nargle pipe

Tobacco

BLACK SEA

Tourism

Cotton

Shish kebab

ANKARA

Carpets

Konya

Tourism

Whirling dervish

TURKEY

Sheep

Goats

HEAD OF HERCULES

Selemiye Mosque
Adana

Harran domed dwellings

Aleppo

Grapes

Nicosia

Cedar

Cotton

Euphrates

SYRIA

Goats

BEIRUT

DAMASCUS

Haifa

Silk

Tel Aviv-Yafo

AMMAN

JERUSALEM

Oranges

JORDAN

Sheep

SINAI DESERT

Aqaba

Bedouin tent

Petra (The Khazneh)

Camels

HEJAZ

AN NAFUD

SAUDI

Coral

Traditional dress

Dates

NEJD

Pearls

Medina

Yanbu

Petrochemicals

RED

Jiddah

THE GREAT MOSQUE
Mecca

Roses

SEA

Sharks

Baboons

Wheat

Barracuda

Coffee

CYPRUS (flag)

SYRIA (flag)

LEBANON (flag)

ISRAEL (flag)

JORDAN (flag)

SAUDI ARABIA (flag)

JERUSALEM

Dome of the Rock

Wailing Wall

Jerusalem is a holy place for Christians, Moslems, and Jews, and it is visited by millions of people each year. The Church of the Holy Sepulchre is built where Christians believe Christ was buried. The gold-topped Dome of the Rock is a mosque built where Moslems believe Mohammed ascended into heaven. The Wailing Wall, where Jews go to pray, is all that remains of the Jewish Temple built by King Herod in the 1st century BC.

FACTS AND FIGURES

Dhow (Arab boat) off the Yemen coast.

Largest city: Tehran (Iran), 8,712,100.

Hottest capital: Riyadh, in Saudi Arabia, is the hottest capital city in the world, with average July temperatures of over 40°C (104°F).

Sand dunes in the Rub al Khali (The Empty Quarter) in Saudi Arabia. Dunes are formed by the wind, which blows the sand into mounds.

BAHRAIN
Capital: Al Manamah
Area: 678 sq km (262 sq miles)

CYPRUS
Capital: Nicosia
Area: 9,251 sq km (3,571 sq miles)

IRAN
Capital: Tehran
Area: 1,648,000 sq km (636,297 sq miles)

IRAQ
Capital: Baghdad
Area: 438,317 sq km (169,235 sq miles)

ISRAEL
Capital: Jerusalem
Area: 20,770 sq km (8,017 sq miles)
Plus the occupied territories of Gaza Strip, Golan Heights, and West Bank, total area 7,418 sq km (2,864 miles)

JORDAN
Capital: Amman
Area: 89,206 sq km (34,443 sq miles)

KUWAIT
Capital: Kuwait
Area: 17,818 sq km (6,879 sq miles)

LEBANON
Capital: Beirut
Area: 10,400 sq km (4,015 sq miles)

OMAN
Capital: Muscat
Area: 212,457 sq km (82,030 sq miles)

QATAR
Capital: Doha
Area: 11,000 sq km (4,247 sq miles)

SAUDI ARABIA
Capital: Riyadh
Area: 2,149,690 sq km (830,001 sq miles)

SYRIA
Capital: Damascus
Area: 185,180 sq km (71,500 sq miles)

TURKEY
Capital: Ankara
Area: 779,452 sq km (300,948 sq miles)

UNITED ARAB EMIRATES
Capital: Abu Dhabi
Area: 83,600 sq km (32,278 sq miles)

YEMEN
Capital: Sana
Area: 527,968 sq km (203,850 sq miles)

SOUTHERN ASIA

THE LARGEST COUNTRY in Southern Asia is India, and the region is often called the "Indian subcontinent". Over one billion people live in Southern Asia – around 22 per cent of the world's total population.

Most people in Southern Asia live in the wetter areas on the coasts and on the fertile plains of the Indus and Ganges rivers. Nearly three-quarters of the people earn their living from farming. Water is vital, and farmers depend on the monsoon rains, which fall between May and November. The most important crop is rice.

India was united in the 16th and 17th centuries under the Mogul emperors. Then, in the 18th century, the country became part of the British Empire. India gained independence from Britain in 1947, when it was divided into two countries with different religions: Moslem Pakistan and Hindu India. In 1971 the eastern part of Pakistan became a separate country, called Bangladesh.

Today Pakistan and India are the most industrial countries in Southern Asia. Pakistan has textile, food processing, and chemical industries. India produces oil, coal, iron ore, manganese, and copper, and has a variety of industries, including iron and steel, car manufacturing, and computers.

Scale:
0 200 400 600 800 Kilometres
0 100 200 300 400 500 Miles

THE TAJ MAHAL

The Taj Mahal was built near Agra in northern India by the Mogul Emperor, Shah Jehan, as a burial place for his wife, the Empress Mumtaz Mahal. It was built between 1630 and 1650 and about 20,000 labourers worked on the building. The Taj Mahal is made of white marble, which was brought 500 km (310 miles) from Rajasthan. The interior is decorated with precious and semi-precious stones.

Map labels

TURKMENISTAN · UZBEKISTAN · TAJIKISTAN

Veiled Afghan women
Carpets
HINDU KUSH
K2 (MT GODWIN AUSTEN) 8,611 m
Snow leopard
KHYBER PASS
Herat
Lapis lazuli
Kabul
AFGHANISTAN
Afghan headgear
Peaches
ISLAMABAD
RHOTAS FORT
Lahore
GOLDEN TEMPLE (AMRITSAR)
Sikh
Bactrian camel
JAMIA MOSQUE (QUETTA)
BADSHAHI MOSQUE
PARLIAMENT HOUSE
IRAN
PAKISTAN
Delhi
NEW DELHI
Camels
Agra
Jaipur
Indus
Cotton
THAR DESERT
TOMB OF MUHAMMAD ALI JINNAH
Hyderabad
PALACE OF THE WINDS
Millet
Sari
Chemicals
Karachi
Wheat
Sheep and goats
Peanuts
INDIA
AFGHANISTAN (flag)
Green turtle
Cars
Dhow (Arab boat)
PAKISTAN (flag)
Cotton
Iron and steel
VICTORIA RAILWAY TERMINUS (BOMBAY)
Cattle
Bombay
Pune
Cotton
Sitar player
Hyderabad
Indian cobra
Pepper
Temple elephant
ARABIAN SEA
Herrings
Bangalore
Coconut palms
MEENAKSHI TEMPLE
Prawns
INDIA (flag)
Sardines

MOUNTAIN PEAKS IN THE HIMALAYAS

MT EVEREST
8,848 m

KANCHENJUNGA
8,586 m

MAKALU I
8,481 m

DHAULAGIRI
8,172 m

NANGA PARBAT
8,126 m

FACTS AND FIGURES

Fishermen at Negombo, Sri Lanka.

Largest metropolitan areas:
Bombay (India), 12,596,000;
Calcutta (India), 11,022,000;
Delhi (India), 7,207,000;
Madras (India), 3,841,000;
Karachi (Pakistan), 8,014,000;
Dhaka (Bangladesh), 3,397,200.

Longest river:
Indus, 2,896 km (1,800 miles).

Largest island: Sri Lanka,
65,610 sq km (25,325 sq miles).

Highest mountains:
Everest (Nepal-China), 8,848 m
(29,028 ft); K2 (Mt Godwin
Austen) (Pakistan-China), 8,611 m
(28,250 ft); Kanchenjunga (India-
Nepal), 8,586 m (28,170 ft).

**World's heaviest recorded
annual rainfall:** Cherrapunji, in
northeast India, received 26.4 m
(1,042 in) of rain between
August 1860 and July 1861.

*Many Nepalese farmers keep yaks,
which are used as pack animals. They
also provide milk, meat, and wool.*

AFGHANISTAN
Capital: Kabul
Area: 652,090 sq km (251,792 sq miles)
Population: 20,500,000

BANGLADESH
Capital: Dhaka
Area: 143,998 sq km (55,602 sq miles)
Population: 122,200,000

BHUTAN
Capital: Thimphu
Area: 47,000 sq km (18,148 sq miles)
Population: 1,700,000

BURMA
Capital: Rangoon (Yangon)
Area: 676,552 sq km (261,237 sq miles)
Population: 44,600,000

INDIA
Capital: New Delhi
Area: 3,287,590 sq km (1,269,437 sq miles)
Population: 896,600,000

NEPAL
Capital: Kathmandu
Area: 140,797 sq km (54,365 sq miles)
Population: 21,100,000

PAKISTAN
Capital: Islamabad
Area: 796,095 sq km (307,396 sq miles)
Population: 128,100,000

SRI LANKA
Capital: Colombo
Area: 65,610 sq km (25,334 sq miles)
Population: 17,900,000

CHINA

Yaks

Red panda

MT EVEREST
8,848 m

HIMALAYAS

NEPAL

KATHMANDU

THIMPHU

Picking tea

BHUTAN

Sugar-cane

Rice

Ganges

Indian rhinoceros

Rubies

Jade

Hauling teak logs

Cycle rickshaw

Dhoti (loincloth)

Ox cart

VICTORIA MEMORIAL

DHAKA

BANGLADESH

BURMA (MYANMAR)

Opium poppy

I N D I A

Calcutta

Mandalay

Tiger

Coal

Rice

PAGAN TEMPLE (ANANDA)

Leg rower

LAOS

Lingaraja Temple

Fishing

BANGLADESH

"Giraffe" necked woman of Padaung

THAILAND

Tobacco

NEPAL

Hindu dancer

Krishna

BHUTAN

SHWE DAGON PADOGA

Buddhist monks

RANGOON (YANGON)

Mackerel

BURMA (MYANMAR)

Rubber trees

Madras

BAY OF BENGAL

ANDAMAN ISLANDS (INDIA)

Lobster

Outrigger fishing boat

SRI LANKA

Picking tea

SRI LANKA

Coconut palms

COLOMBO

NICOBAR ISLANDS (INDIA)

THAILAND

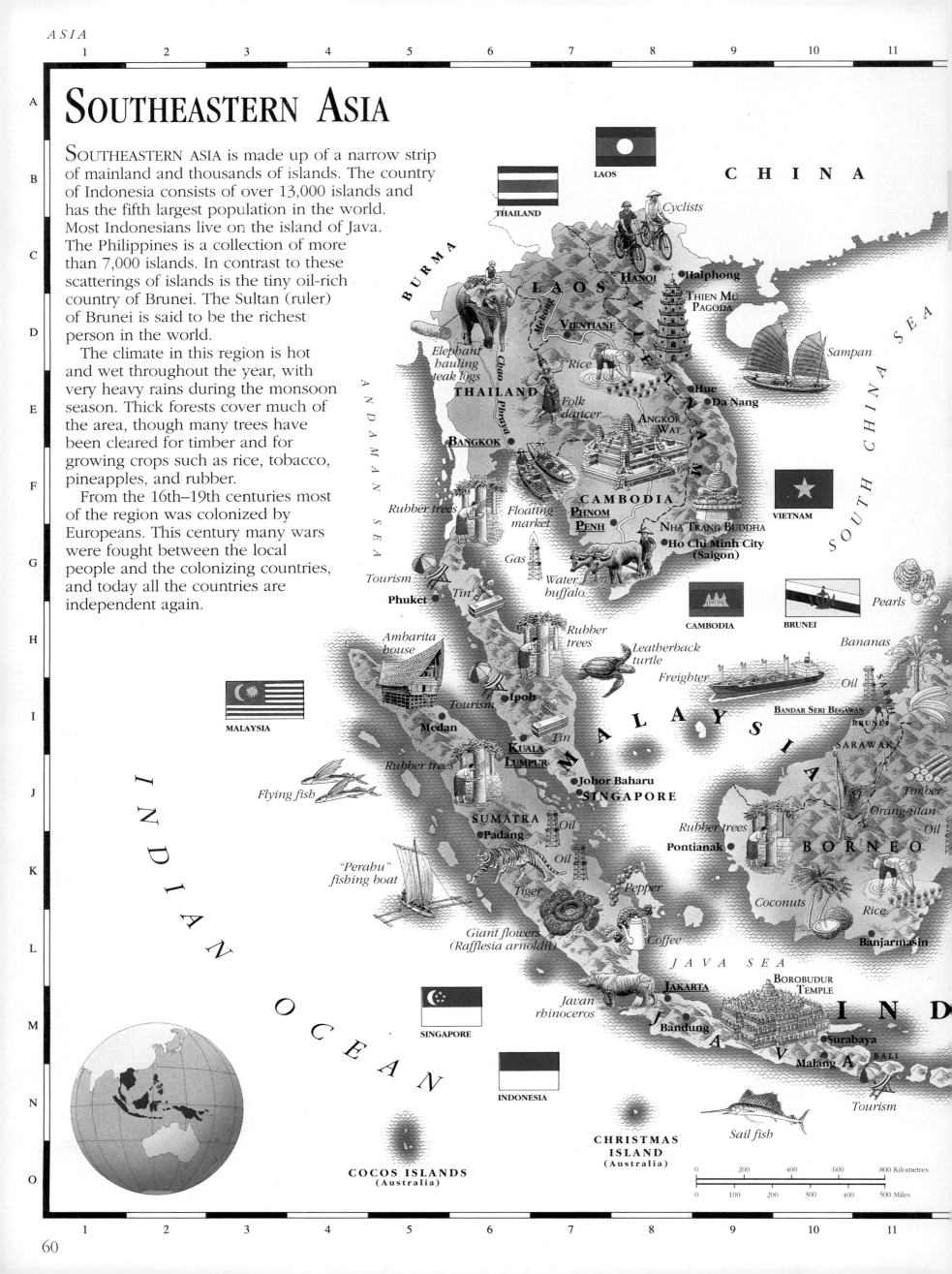

SOUTHEASTERN ASIA

SOUTHEASTERN ASIA is made up of a narrow strip of mainland and thousands of islands. The country of Indonesia consists of over 13,000 islands and has the fifth largest population in the world. Most Indonesians live on the island of Java. The Philippines is a collection of more than 7,000 islands. In contrast to these scatterings of islands is the tiny oil-rich country of Brunei. The Sultan (ruler) of Brunei is said to be the richest person in the world.

The climate in this region is hot and wet throughout the year, with very heavy rains during the monsoon season. Thick forests cover much of the area, though many trees have been cleared for timber and for growing crops such as rice, tobacco, pineapples, and rubber.

From the 16th–19th centuries most of the region was colonized by Europeans. This century many wars were fought between the local people and the colonizing countries, and today all the countries are independent again.

LAOS

THAILAND

CHINA

Cyclists

BURMA

LAOS

Haiphong

Hanoi

Thien Mu Pagoda

VIENTIANE

Elephant hauling teak logs

Rice

SOUTH CHINA SEA

Sampan

Chao Phraya

THAILAND

Folk dancer

Hue

Da Nang

ANGKOR WAT

BANGKOK

CAMBODIA

VIETNAM

ANDAMAN SEA

Rubber trees

Floating market

PHNOM PENH

Nha Trang Buddha

Ho Chi Minh City (Saigon)

Gas

Water buffalo

CAMBODIA

BRUNEI

Pearls

Tourism

Phuket

Tin

Bananas

Leatherback turtle

Freighter

Oil

Rubber trees

Ambarita house

Tourism

Ipoh

BANDAR SERI BEGAWAN

BRUNEI

MALAYSIA

Medan

Tin

SABAH

SARAWAK

Rubber trees

MALAYSIA

Kuala Lumpur

Rubber trees

Timber

Orang-utan

Johor Baharu

SINGAPORE

Flying fish

SUMATRA

Padang

Oil

Oil

Pontianak

Oil

BORNEO

INDIAN OCEAN

"Perahu" fishing boat

Tiger

Oil

Pepper

Coconuts

Rice

Giant flowers (Rafflesia arnoldii)

Coffee

Banjarmasin

JAVA SEA

SINGAPORE

Javan rhinoceros

JAKARTA

BOROBUDUR TEMPLE

IND

Bandung

JAVA

BALI

Surabaya

Malang

INDONESIA

CHRISTMAS ISLAND (Australia)

Sail fish

Tourism

COCOS ISLANDS (Australia)

| 0 | 200 | 400 | 600 | 800 Kilometres |
| 0 | 100 | 200 | 300 | 400 | 500 Miles |

FACTS AND FIGURES

Planting rice in Malaysia. Seedlings are transplanted to a flooded field after they have grown in a nursery.

Largest cities:
Jakarta (Indonesia), 9,000,000;
Manila (Philippines), 7,729,000;
Bangkok (Thailand), 5,875,900;
Ho Chi Minh City (Vietnam, previously called Saigon), 4,075,700.

Highest mountain: Puncak Jaya (Indonesia), 5,030 m (16,503 ft).

Largest island: New Guinea, 808,510 sq km (312,168 sq miles).

Longest river:
Mekong, 4,184 km (2,600 miles).

Longest name in the world:
The Thai name for Bangkok is Krungthep maha nakorn, amarn rattanakosindra, mahindrayudhya, mahadilok pop noparatana rajdhani mahasathan, amorn piman avatarn satit, sakkatultiya visanukarn prasit.

BRUNEI
Capital: Bandar Seri Begawan
Area: 5,765 sq km (2,225 sq miles)
Population: 300,000
Languages: Malay, English
Religion: Moslem

CAMBODIA
Capital: Phnom Pénh
Area: 181,035 sq km (69,881 sq miles)
Population: 9,000,000
Language: Khmer
Religion: Buddhist

INDONESIA
Capital: Jakarta
Area: 1,904,569 sq km (735,412 sq miles)
Population: 194,600,000
Language: Indonesian
Religion: Moslem

LAOS
Capital: Vientiane
Area: 236,800 sq km (91,435 sq miles)
Population: 4,600,000
Languages: Lao, French
Religion: Buddhist

MALAYSIA
Capital: Kuala Lumpur
Area: 329,749 sq km (127,326 sq miles)
Population: 19,200,000
Languages: Malay, English, Chinese
Religions: Moslem, Buddhist

PAPUA NEW GUINEA
Capital: Port Moresby
Area: 462,840 sq km (178,716 sq miles)
Population: 4,100,000
Languages: English, numerous others
Religion: Christian

PHILIPPINES
Capital: Manila
Area: 300,000 sq km (115,839 sq miles)
Population: 66,500,000
Languages: Pilipino, English, Spanish
Religions: Christian, Moslem

SINGAPORE
Capital: Singapore City
Area: 618 sq km (239 sq miles)
Population: 2,800,000
Languages: Malay, Chinese, English
Religions: Taoist, Buddhist

THAILAND
Capital: Bangkok
Area: 513,115 sq km (198,129 sq miles)
Population: 56,900,000
Language: Thai
Religion: Buddhist

VIETNAM
Capital: Hanoi
Area: 329,558 sq km (127,252 sq miles)
Population: 70,900,000
Languages: Vietnamese, French, Chinese
Religion: Buddhist

SINGAPORE

Singapore is a small island, just 40 km (25 miles) long by 25 km (15.5 miles) wide. It is an independent nation and one of the world's most important ports and trading centres. Many different races live in Singapore. Three-quarters of the population are Chinese, with smaller numbers of Malays and Indians. The remainder are Europeans, Arabs, or Japanese. These people all celebrate different festivals, making Singapore a lively and colourful place throughout the year.

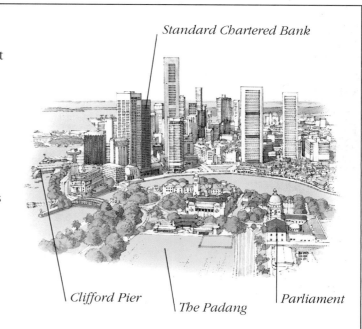

Standard Chartered Bank

Clifford Pier

The Padang

Parliament

PACIFIC OCEAN

Rice terrraces

MANILA

LUZON

PHILIPPINES

Sugar cane

Cebu

PHILIPPINES

Monkey-eating eagle

Coral reefs

MINDANAO

Davao

Zamboanga

Vinta boat

Coral reefs

CELEBES SEA

Coconuts

Sago palms

Sago palms

Toraja house

CELEBES

MOLUCCAS

Oil

Shrimps

Nutmeg

Oil

Tuna

Spirit house

Coconuts

Jayapura

SERAM SEA

SERAM

IRIAN JAYA

PAPUA NEW GUINEA

NEW BRITAIN

Cloves

Coffee

△ Puncak Jaya 5,030 m

△ Mt Wilhelm 4,509 m

Ujung Pandang

BANDA SEA

Crabs

Tree kangaroo

Irian Jaya native

PAPUA

Dancer and drum

ONESIA

Bird of paradise

PORT MORESBY

Komodo dragon

Asmat warriors

FLORES

Maize

TIMOR

ARAFURA SEA

SUMBA

Kupang

PAPUA NEW GUINEA

TIMOR SEA

AUSTRALIA

CHINA AND NORTHEASTERN ASIA

MORE PEOPLE live in China than in any other country. China has over one billion inhabitants, and one person in every five in the world is Chinese. China is also the world's third largest country, after the Russian Federation and Canada. Most people live in the east of China, where the climate is wet and the land is good for farming. In most places the land is owned by each village, and everyone works on it together, sharing the harvest.

Tibet lies in the highlands of southwest China at an average height of 4,500 m (14,800 ft) above sea level. This is higher than most mountains in Europe and the United States. The Himalayas, the world's highest mountains, stretch along the border with India.

After a long civil war in China, a communist government was formed in 1949, led by Mao Zedong. The defeated nationalists set up a rival Republic of China on the small island of Taiwan, which is still independent. The small province of Hong Kong is at present a British colony, but it will become part of China in 1997. In Korea, a war was fought between communist and non-communist forces. Korea is now divided into two countries, North and South Korea.

THE FORBIDDEN CITY

On one side of the central square in China's capital city, Beijing (Peking), is Tiananmen Gate, the Gate of Heavenly Peace. Through it lies the old city where the Chinese emperors had their court from 1421 to 1911. It was known as the Forbidden City because ordinary people were not allowed to enter, but today it is open to the public. At its heart the Imperial Palace is surrounded by a high wall and a water-filled moat.

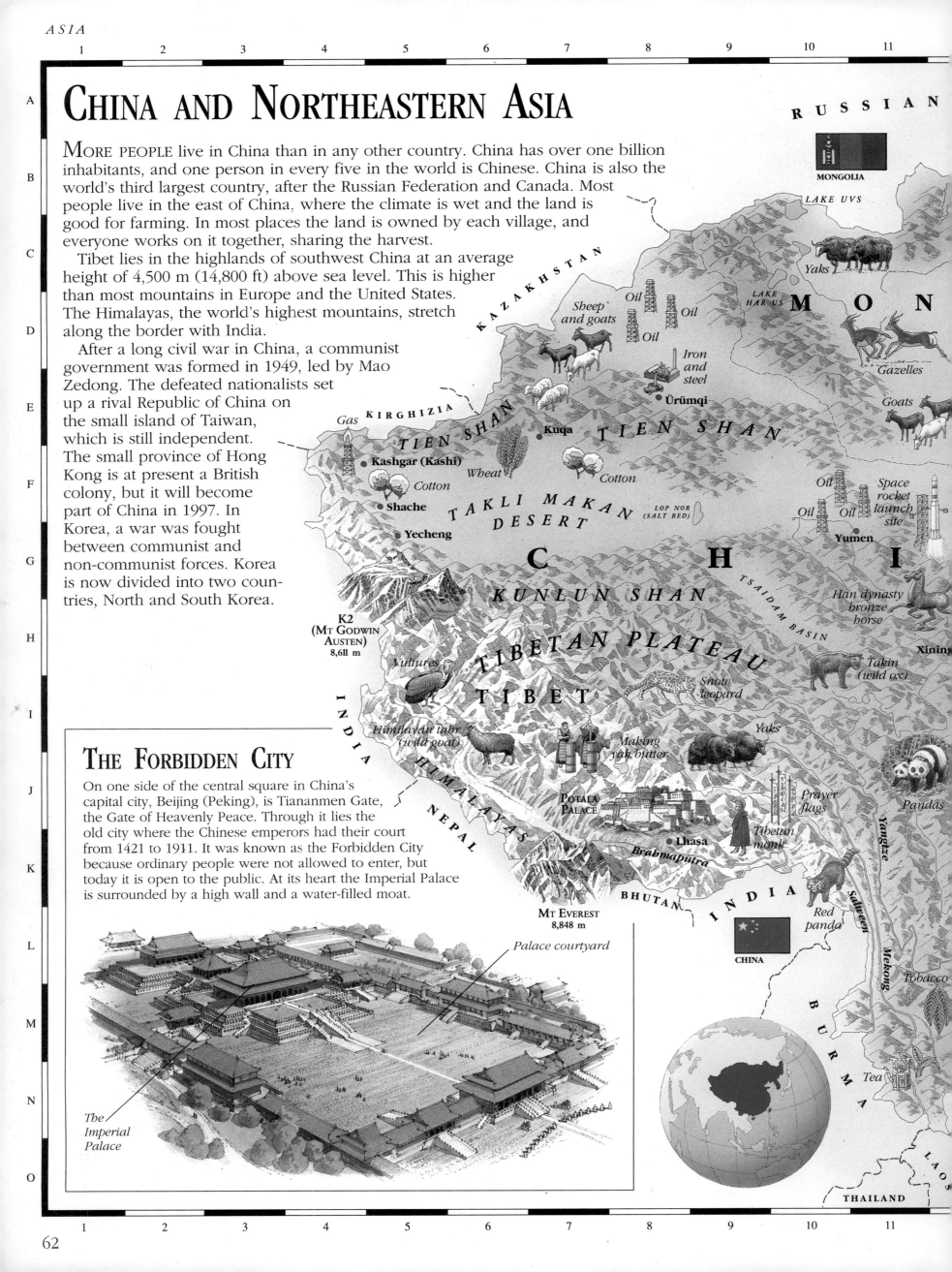

RUSSIAN

MONGOLIA

LAKE UVS

Yaks

KAZAKHSTAN

LAKE HAR US

M O N

Gazelles

Sheep and goats

Oil

Oil

Oil

Iron and steel

Goats

Ürümqi

Gas

KIRGHIZIA

TIEN SHAN

Kuqa

TIEN SHAN

Wheat

Cotton

Kashgar (Kashi)

Cotton

TAKLI MAKAN DESERT

LOP NOR (SALT BED)

Oil

Space rocket launch site

Shache

Oil

Oil

Yecheng

Yumen

C H I

K2 (MT GODWIN AUSTEN) 8,611 m

KUNLUN SHAN

TSAIDAM BASIN

Han dynasty bronze horse

Vultures

TIBETAN PLATEAU

Takin (wild ox)

Xining

INDIA

Himalayan tahr (wild goat)

TIBET

Snow leopard

Yaks

Making yak butter

HIMALAYAS

POTALA PALACE

Prayer flags

Pandas

NEPAL

Lhasa

Tibetan monk

Brahmaputra

BHUTAN

INDIA

Yangtze

Red panda

MT EVEREST 8,848 m

CHINA

Salween

Tobacco

Palace courtyard

The Imperial Palace

Mekong

BURMA

Tea

LAOS

THAILAND

13　　　14　　　15　　　16　　　17　　　18　　　19　　　20　　　21　　　22　　　23

FEDERATION

GOLIA

Sheep
ULAN BATOR
Gers (Mongol tents)

GOBI DESERT

Bactrian camels

Cowboy and wild horse

LAKE HULUN

Kaoliang (cereal crop)

Coal

Qiqihar

Vehicles

Songhua

Coal

Oil

Harbin

Tiger

INNER MONGOLIA

Goats

Soya beans

Oil

Vehicles

Changchun

Jilin

Iron and steel

Locomotives

Iron and steel

Baotou

TEMPLE OF HEAVEN

Wheat

Coal

Oil

Fushun

Shenyang

Anshan

Maize

NORTH KOREA

Diesel locomotives

GREAT WALL OF CHINA

N A

BEIJING (PEKING)

Dalian (Luda)

PYONGYANG

SEOUL

Electronics and vehicles

Sheep

Yinchuan

Vuwei

Tianjin

Shipbuilding

SEA OF JAPAN

Cyclists

Oil

YELLOW SEA

SOUTH KOREA

Fish

Taiyuan

Jinan

Iron and steel

Millet

Maize

Qingdao

Fish

Shipbuilding

Lanzhou

TERRACOTTA ARMY

Cotton

Vehicles

Yellow River

Wheat

KOREA STRAIT

NORTH KOREA

Chemicals and textiles

Luoyang

Zhengzhou

Planting rice

Xi'an

Sweet potatoes

Ducks

Porcelain

Tobacco

Yangtze

Nanjing

Shipbuilding

SOUTH KOREA

Oil

Oil

Yunxian

Iron and steel

Cotton

Shanghai

EAST CHINA SEA

Chengdu

Maize

Cotton

Wuhan

Hangzhou

Fish

Yangtze

Rice

Fishing

Millet

Nanxian

Goldfish

Chongqing

Nanchang

Wenzhou

Chemicals and vehicles

Junk

Tea

Silk

Guiyang

Changsha

Nanping

Limestone hills

Sweet potatoes

Fuzhou

Water buffalo plough

Pigs

Ganzhou

Kunming

Guilin

Planting rice

Sugar cane

TAIPEI

Liuzhou

Sampan

Shantou

TAIWAN

PHILIPPINE SEA

Mengzi

Canton (Guangzhou)

Chaoyang

Malipo

Skyscrapers of modern Hong Kong

Nanning

HONG KONG

MACAU

VIETNAM

Gibbons

Sugar cane

Shellfish

TAIWAN

Rubber trees

Junk fishing

SOUTH CHINA SEA

HAINAN

0　200　400　600　800 Kilometres
0　100　200　300　400　500 Miles

FACTS AND FIGURES

The Great Wall of China was built to protect the country's northern border against invaders. It is nearly 3,460 km (2,150 miles) long.

Longest river:
Yangtze (Chang Jiang), 6,300 km (3,915 miles).

Largest city population:
Shanghai (China), 13,510,000.

Gateway to the Chaotain Palace, one of many historic buildings in Nanjing, formerly the capital of China.

CHINA
Capital: Beijing (Peking)
Area: 9,596,961 sq km (3,704,440 miles)
Population: 1,205,200,000
Languages: Chinese
Religions: Confucianism, Buddhism, Taoism, Moslem
Currency: Yuan
Government: Communist republic

HONG KONG
Capital: Victoria
Area: 1,045 sq km (403 sq miles)
Population: 5,800,000
Languages: English and Chinese
Religions: Buddhism, Christianity, Taoism
Currency: Hong Kong dollar
Government: British colony

MACAU
Capital: Macau
Area: 16 sq km (6 sq miles)
Population: 487,000
Languages: Portuguese and Chinese
Religions: Buddhism, Christianity, Taoism
Currency: Pataca
Government: Portuguese colony

MONGOLIA
Capital: Ulan Bator
Area: 1,565,000 sq km (604,247 sq miles)
Population: 2,400,000
Language: Mongolian
Religions: Buddhism, Lamaism, Moslem
Currency: Tugrik
Government: Republic

NORTH KOREA
Capital: Pyongyang
Area: 120,538 sq km (46,540 sq miles)
Population: 23,100,000
Language: Korean
Religions: Buddhism, Confucianism, Taoism
Currency: North Korean Won
Government: Communist republic

SOUTH KOREA
Capital: Seoul
Area: 99,016 sq km (38,230 sq miles)
Population: 44,500,000
Language: Korean
Religions: Buddhism, Christianity, Confucianism
Currency: South Korean Won
Government: Republic

TAIWAN
Capital: Taipei
Area: 35,990 sq km (13,890 sq miles)
Population: 20,800,000
Language: Chinese
Religions: Buddhism, Taoism, Christianity
Currency: New Taiwan dollar
Government: Republic

13　　　　16　　　17　　　18　　　19　　　20　　　21　　　22　　　23

JAPAN

JAPAN is made up of four main islands – called Hokkaido, Honshu, Shikoku, and Kyushu – and thousands of smaller ones. The country lies to the east of the main part of Asia. This is an area where two plates of the Earth's crust meet, making earthquakes common. Nearly three-quarters of the country is mountainous and wooded. There is little land suitable for agriculture, but what there is is farmed very efficiently. The main crop is rice. Because much of the land cannot be farmed for food, the Japanese eat a lot of fish, and Japan catches more fish than any other nation.

Japan's 122 million people live on the small amount of flat land, mostly on the coasts. In these populated areas there is a very dense concentration of people and activity. Most of the people live in the great cities on the south coast of Honshu island, such as Nagoya, Tokyo, and Osaka.

In the last 40 years Japan has become one of the world's most important industrial nations. This is all the more remarkable because the oil and most of the raw materials that are needed to make the goods have to be imported into the country. Japanese cars, electrical goods, ships, cameras, and many other products are exported all over the world.

KYOTO

Kyoto lies on the island of Honshu. It is one of Japan's largest cities and an important cultural centre. For more than 1,000 years it was the capital city of Japan. It has many historic treasures, including shrines, temples, gardens, and ancient buildings. It is Japan's most popular tourist centre and about 20 million people visit the city every year.

Map labels

KURIL ISLANDS
Nemuro
Trout
Kushiro
Pollock
Steller's sea eagle
Ceremonial Ainu dress
Japanese crane
Teshio
HOKKAIDO
Paper
Brown bear
Coal
Potatoes
Timber
Fish oil
Snow festival
Sapporo
Muroran
Fishing boats
Cod
Hakodate
MT YOTEI 1,107 m
Halibut
JAPAN
Saury
Mackerel
Oysters
Crab
Apples
Bonsai (miniature trees)
Morioka
Judo
Japanese arts
Sendai
Coal
Aomori
Sake
Rice planting
Fukushima
Akita
Fish flags (carp streamers)
Anchovies
Sardines
HONSHU
SADO ISLAND
JAPAN
OCEAN

Skyscrapers of modern Tokyo

Hitachi

Electronics

Tuna

Macaque

TOKYO

Electronics

Kawasaki
Yokohama

BRONZE
BUDDHA
(KAMAKURA)

IZU ISLANDS

Shizuoka

Cherry blossom

Nagano

Skiing

Serow

Mt Fuji
3,776 m

Tea
terraces

Toyama

Cars

Nagoya

Pearls

NAGOYA
CASTLE

Bullet
train

Fukui

Sumo wrestler

Terraced
rice fields

Kyoto

GOLD PAVILION

Osaka

Iron
and steel

Kobe

Shipbuilding

Citrus fruits

Sardines

Fishing
boats

Squid

Shinto
dignitary

Tottori

Okayama

Satsumas

Squid

Crab

Oil
tanker

OKI
ISLANDS

Shinto
shrine

Torii gate

Hiroshima

MATSUYAMA
CASTLE

SHIKOKU

Kochi

Loggerhead
turtle

Shrimps

Kabuki
theatre

Kitakyushu

Iron
and steel

Chemicals

Kumamoto

Rice
planting

Miyazaki

Tofu
(bean curd)

Sweet
potatoes

OSUMI
ISLANDS

Anchovies

TSUSHIMA
ISLANDS

IKI

Fukuoka

Pottery

Nagasaki

KYUSHU

Kagoshima

Octopus

GOTO
ISLANDS

Shellfish

EAST CHINA SEA

Mackerel

SEA OF JAPAN

A typical Japanese garden in Hiroshima.

Tokyo, Japan's capital, and a major industrial port.

Temple statue at Nikko, Honshu.

JAPAN
Capital: Tokyo
Area: 377,801 sq km (145,835 sq miles)
Population: 125,000,000
Language: Japanese
Religions: Shintoism, Buddhism
Currency: Yen

FACTS AND FIGURES

Four largest islands: Honshu, Hokkaido, Kyushu, Shikoku. There are also about 4,000 small islands.

Highest mountain: Mt Fuji, 3,776 m (12,388 ft).

Main ports: Tokyo, Yokohama, Osaka, and Kobe.

Wettest area: All of Japan has high rainfall, but the wettest place is the southernmost island of Kyushu, where average rainfall reaches over 2,200 mm (86.6 in) per year.

Coldest area: Hokkaido has average winter temperatures of -10°C (14°F).

Longest railway tunnel in the world: The Seikan Rail Tunnel in Japan runs for 53.85 km (33.46 miles) between Tappi Saki on Honshu island and Fukushima on Hokkaido.

World's largest fishing fleet: Japan catches around 14 per cent of the total world catch – more than any other country. Each Japanese person eats an average of 30 kg (65 lbs) of fish a year.

World's tallest lighthouse: The steel lighthouse in Yokohama, Japan is 106 m (348 ft) high. It can be seen from 32 km (20 miles) away.

Food: Only 15 per cent of the land, mostly on the coastal plains, can be farmed. But despite this, Japan is 70 per cent self-sufficient in food.

World's top oil importer: Japan. The *Seawise Giant*, a Japanese tanker built in 1981, is the largest tanker in the world. It is almost 500 m (547 yards) long and can carry 565,000 tonnes of crude oil.

Largest cities: Tokyo, 7,976,000; Yokohama, 3,233,000; Osaka, 2,506,000; Nagoya, 2,098,000; Sapporo, 1,687,000; Kyoto, 1,339,000; Kobe, 1,459,000; Fukuoka, 1,142,000.

200 Kilometres
125 Miles

AFRICA

The Muhammad Ali mosque in Cairo, Egypt.

AFRICA, the world's second largest continent, stretches about 4,000 km (2,500 miles) north and south of the Equator. It is the warmest of all the continents. The only permanent snow and ice are found on the peaks of the highest mountains, such as Mount Kenya and Mount Kilimanjaro. In the regions near the Equator, the hot and wet climate supports the dense jungle vegetation of the tropical rainforest. Today much of the forest has been cleared for farming and timber.

Moving away from the Equator, the climate becomes increasingly dry, and the forest gives way to tropical grassland, called savannah. For thousands of years the savannah has supported huge herds of plant-eating animals – gazelles, wildebeest, zebras, elephants, and giraffes – along with the predators who hunt and feed on them – lions, leopards, and hyenas. Today farming has greatly reduced the size of the herds, and some animals, such as the African elephant, are in danger of being wiped out forever.

Still farther to the north and south lie the great deserts, where the climate is so dry that few plants

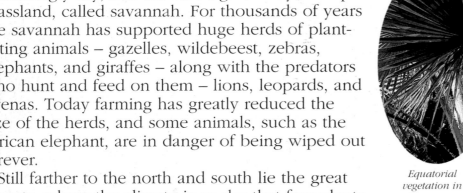

Equatorial vegetation in Cameroon.

and animals can survive. Northern Africa is dominated by the Sahara, the world's largest desert. In the south lie the Kalahari and Namib deserts.

Africa is an immense plateau, broken by a few mountain ranges. In some areas a narrow coastal plain stretches along the edge of the plateau. Cutting across East Africa is the Great Rift Valley, with its many lakes and volcanoes. This long valley was formed centuries ago when land slipped down between huge cracks in the Earth's crust. Some scientists believe that the land east of the Rift Valley will eventually break away from Africa and become a new continent, just as the Red Sea marks the place where Arabia once split away from the rest of Africa.

Off the east coast of Africa lies the island of Madagascar, which broke away from Africa over 50 million years ago. Because of the island's isolation, unique plants and animals have evolved there. Twenty species of lemur, an animal distantly related to the monkey, are only found there.

Open cast mining in South Africa.

FACTS ABOUT AFRICA

Area: 30,335,000 sq km (11,712,434 sq miles).

Population: 701,990,000.

Number of independent countries: 54 (the most on any continent).

Largest countries: Sudan, 2,500,000 sq km (967,500 sq miles); Algeria, 2,381,741 sq km (919,597 sq miles).

Most populated countries: Nigeria, 119,300,000; Egypt, 56,100,000; Ethiopia, 51,300,000.

Largest metropolitan areas: Cairo (Egypt), 6,452,000; Alexandria (Egypt), 3,295,000; Kinshasa (Zaire), 2,796,000.

Highest mountains: Kilimanjaro (Tanzania), 5,896 m (19,344 ft); Mt Kenya (Kenya), 5,199 m (17,057 ft); Mt Margherita (Uganda-Zaire), 5,110 m (16,763 ft); Ras Dashen (Ethiopia), 4,620 m (15,158 ft).

Longest rivers: Nile, 6,670 km (4,145 miles), the longest in the world; Zaire, 4,667 km (2,900 miles); Niger, 4,184 km (2,600 miles); Zambezi, 2,735 km (1,700 miles).

Largest lakes: Lake Victoria, 69,400 sq km (26,800 sq miles); Lake Tanganyika, 32,900 sq km (12,102 sq miles); Lake Nyasa, 28,750 sq km (11,100 sq miles); Lake Chad, area varies from 10,000-26,000 sq km (4,000-10,000 sq miles), according to the seasons.

Main deserts: Sahara (the largest in the world), about 9,000,000 sq km (3,474,927 sq miles); Kalahari, about 517,998 sq km (200,000 sq miles).

Largest islands: Madagascar, 587,041 sq km (226,658 sq miles); Réunion, 2,510 sq km (969 sq miles).

World's highest sand dunes: Dunes in the Sahara Desert can be up to 5 km (3 miles) long and 430 m (1,410 ft) high.

World's highest temperature: In 1922 the temperature in Al'Azizya (Libya) reached 58°C (136.4°F) in the shade.

World's largest man-made lake: Lake Volta (Ghana), which was formed by the Akosombo Dam, has a surface area of 8,482 sq km (3,275 miles).

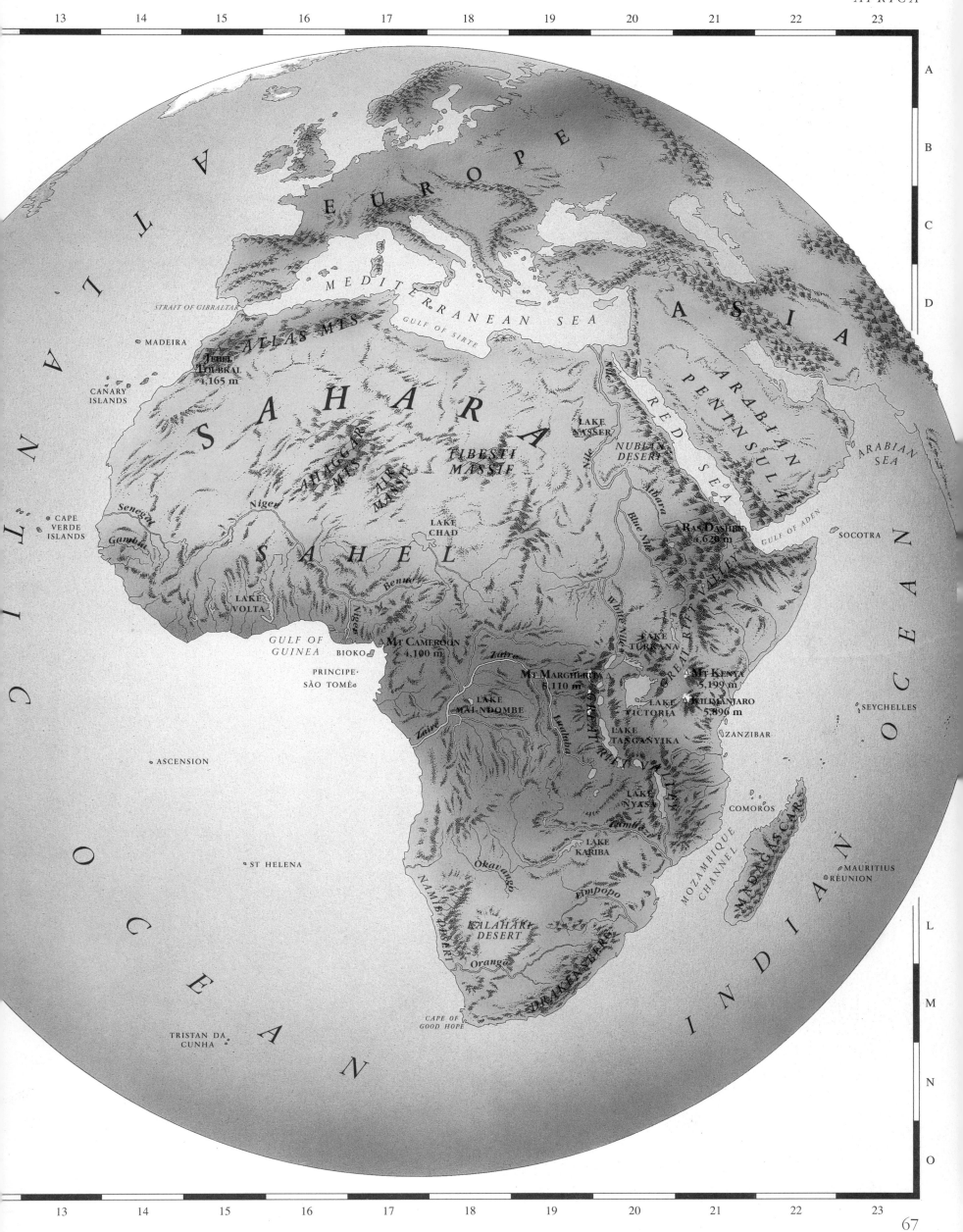

13 14 15 16 17 18 19 20 21 22 23

A
B
C
D

EUROPE

ASIA

ATLANTIC

MEDITERRANEAN SEA

STRAIT OF GIBRALTAR

GULF OF SIRTE

MADEIRA

ATLAS MTS

JEBEL
TOUBKAL
4,165 m

CANARY
ISLANDS

SAHARA

AHAGGAR
MTS

AÏR
MASSIF

TIBESTI
MASSIF

LAKE
NASSER

Nile

NUBIAN
DESERT

Atbara

ARABIAN
PENINSULA

RED SEA

ARABIAN
SEA

CAPE
VERDE
ISLANDS

Senegal

Niger

Gambia

LAKE
CHAD

Blue Nile

RAS DASHEN
4,620 m

GULF OF ADEN

SOCOTRA

SAHEL

Benue

Niger

LAKE
VOLTA

GULF OF
GUINEA

BIOKO

MT CAMEROON
4,100 m

Zaïre

White Nile

LAKE
TURKANA

GREAT RIFT VALLEY

PRINCIPE·
SÃO TOMÉ

MT MARGHERITA
5,110 m

MT KENYA
5,199 m

KILIMANJARO
5,896 m

LAKE
MAI-NDOMBE

Zaïre

LAKE
VICTORIA

SEYCHELLES

ZANZIBAR

ASCENSION

Lualaba

LAKE
TANGANYIKA

COMOROS

ST HELENA

LAKE
NYASA

Zambezi

MADAGASCAR

MOZAMBIQUE
CHANNEL

LAKE
KARIBA

MAURITIUS

RÉUNION

Okavango

Limpopo

NAMIB DESERT

KALAHARI
DESERT

Orange

DRAKENSBERG

INDIAN

OCEAN

L
M

TRISTAN DA
CUNHA

CAPE OF
GOOD HOPE

N
O

OCEAN

13 14 15 16 17 18 19 20 21 22 23

NORTHERN AFRICA

DOMINATING NORTHERN AFRICA is the huge expanse of the Sahara Desert. The climate is wetter along parts of the north coasts, and here citrus fruits, grapes, and dates are grown. Along the Mediterranean coastline tourism is increasingly important. The largest countries in Northern Africa are Egypt and Sudan, both farming countries, and Libya and Algeria, which have rich supplies of oil and natural gas.

The few people who live in the Sahara Desert are mostly nomads, who move from place to place with their sheep and camels. Along the southern edge of the Sahara is an area of semi-desert called the Sahel, which stretches across the countries of Mauritania, Mali, Burkina, Niger, and Chad. These are among the world's poorest countries. In recent years the people there have suffered terrible famines.

West Africa, which includes the countries of Nigeria, Ghana, Benin and Ivory Coast, is a fertile region in which such crops as coffee, groundnuts, and cocoa are grown.

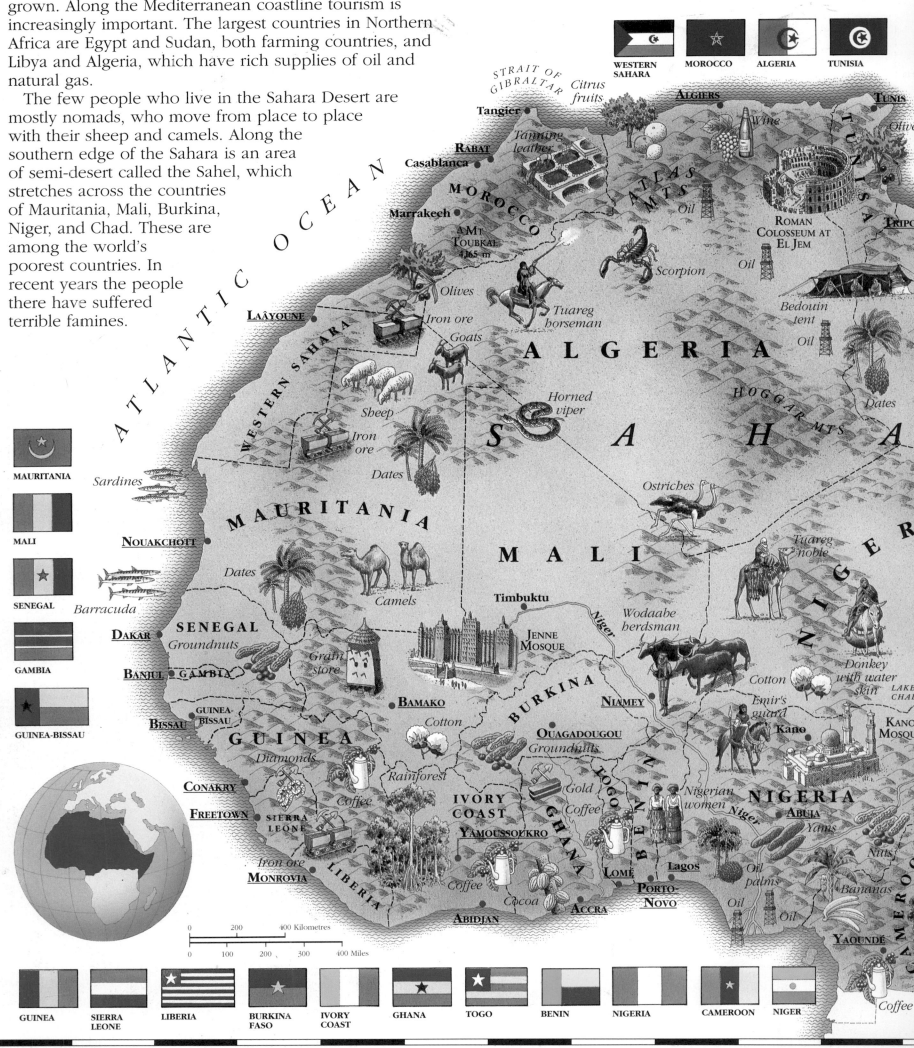

WESTERN SAHARA **MOROCCO** **ALGERIA** **TUNISIA**

MAURITANIA

MALI

SENEGAL

GAMBIA

GUINEA-BISSAU

GUINEA **SIERRA LEONE** **LIBERIA** **BURKINA FASO** **IVORY COAST** **GHANA** **TOGO** **BENIN** **NIGERIA** **CAMEROON** **NIGER**

THE PYRAMIDS AND SPHINX

The pyramids of ancient Egypt were built in about 2500 BC to contain the mummified bodies of pharaohs, or kings. The three largest are at Giza. The Great Pyramid contains more than two million stone blocks. The Sphinx was probably built to guard the Pharaoh Chephren's body.

Pyramid of Chephren

Great Pyramid of Cheops

Pyramid of Mycerinus

FACTS AND FIGURES

Port Said lies at the entrance to the Suez Canal, which links the Mediterranean and Red Seas.

Longest river: Nile, 6,670 km (4,145 miles).

Highest mountain: Ras Dashen (Ethiopia), 4,620 m (15,158 ft).

Largest lake: Lake Chad, area varies from 10,000–26,000 sq km (4,000–10,000 sq miles) according to the season.

ALGERIA
Capital: Algiers

BENIN
Capital: Porto-Novo

BURKINA
Capital: Ouagadougou

CAMEROON
Capital: Yaoundé

CENTRAL AFRICAN REPUBLIC
Capital: Bangui

CHAD
Capital: N'Djamena

DJIBOUTI
Capital: Djibouti

EGYPT
Capital: Cairo

ERITREA
Capital: Asmara

ETHIOPIA
Capital: Addis Ababa

GAMBIA
Capital: Banjul

GHANA
Capital: Accra

GUINEA
Capital: Conakry

GUINEA-BISSAU
Capital: Bissau

IVORY COAST
Capital: Yamoussoukro

LIBERIA
Capital: Monrovia

LIBYA
Capital: Tripoli

MALI
Capital: Bamako

MAURITANIA
Capital: Nouakchott

MOROCCO
Capital: Rabat

NIGER
Capital: Niamey

NIGERIA
Capital: Abuja

SENEGAL
Capital: Dakar

SIERRA LEONE
Capital: Freetown

SOMALIA
Capital: Mogadishu

SUDAN
Capital: Khartoum

TOGO
Capital: Lomé

TUNISIA
Capital: Tunis

WESTERN SAHARA
Capital: Laâyoune

ERITREA

MEDITERRANEAN SEA

Benghazi
Alexandria
Port Said
CAIRO
SINAI
Oil

Olives
Oil
Dates
Oil
Oil

Citrus fruits

PYRAMIDS AT GIZA

EGYPT

Dates
Nile
Cotton

Felucca (Egyptian boat)

LAKE NASSER

L I B Y A

Dates
Jerboa

S A H A R A

Striped hyena

THE GREAT TEMPLE AT ABU SIMBEL

TIBESTI MASSIF

NUBIAN DESERT

Nile DESERT

Nile crocodile

Port Sudan

PYRAMIDS AT MEROE

ERITREA

C H A D

Nomadic caravan
Dates

S U D A N

ASMARA
RAS DASHEN 4,620 m

Hippopotami

Ostriches

KHARTOUM

Coffee

Dhow (Arab boat)

GULF OF ADEN

N'DJAMENA

Groundnuts

Sugar cane

White Nile
Blue Nile

Cheetah

Nuba five-turret dwelling

DJIBOUTI
DJIBOUTI

Chari
Logone

Rhinoceros

Nuba tribesmen

Nomadic tribesman

Cotton

Frankincense (Boswellia tree)

Cotton

CENTRAL AFRICAN REPUBLIC

BANGUI

Diamonds

Elephant

Thatched huts of the Nuer tribe

ADDIS ABABA

Great white pelican

E T H I O P I A

Goats

Oryx

Rainforest

Acacia tree

Lions

S O M A L I A

Giraffes

MOGADISHU

INDIAN OCEAN

Bananas

CENTRAL AFRICAN REPUBLIC
CHAD
LIBYA
EGYPT
SUDAN
ETHIOPIA
DJIBOUTI
SOMALIA

69

SOUTHERN AFRICA

SOUTHERN AFRICA contains a great variety of peoples and landscapes. In the northwest lies the rainforest of the Zaire Basin. To the east lie the high grasslands of East Africa, where the peaks of Mt Kenya and Mt Kilimanjaro are snow-capped all year long and large herds of wild animals still roam the plains. The countries of Kenya, Uganda, and Tanzania contain rich farmland where coffee, tea, maize, and cotton are grown.

Angola, Zambia, and Zimbabwe are rich in diamonds, iron, and copper. Farther south lies the Kalahari Desert, which covers much of Botswana and Namibia. The world's richest diamond and gold mines are in South Africa. This country is also a major producer of fruit, wheat, cotton, and tobacco.

Much of southern Africa developed independently of the rest of the world. But from the late 1880s African culture was seriously disrupted when European nations took control of the region. Since 1959 Africans have regained their independence, except in South Africa where, in 1948, the government introduced a policy of apartheid (an Afrikaans word meaning "apartness"). This separated people according to their colour, and gave power to the white population only. Since 1990 apartheid has begun to crumble.

THE GREAT RIFT VALLEY

The Great Rift Valley is the largest crack in the Earth's crust, stretching 8,700 km (5,400 miles) from Syria in the north, through the Red Sea to Mozambique in southern Africa. It is in East Africa that the scenery of the Rift Valley is most spectacular. In Kenya the walls of the valley rise almost straight up for 1,250 m (4,000 ft).

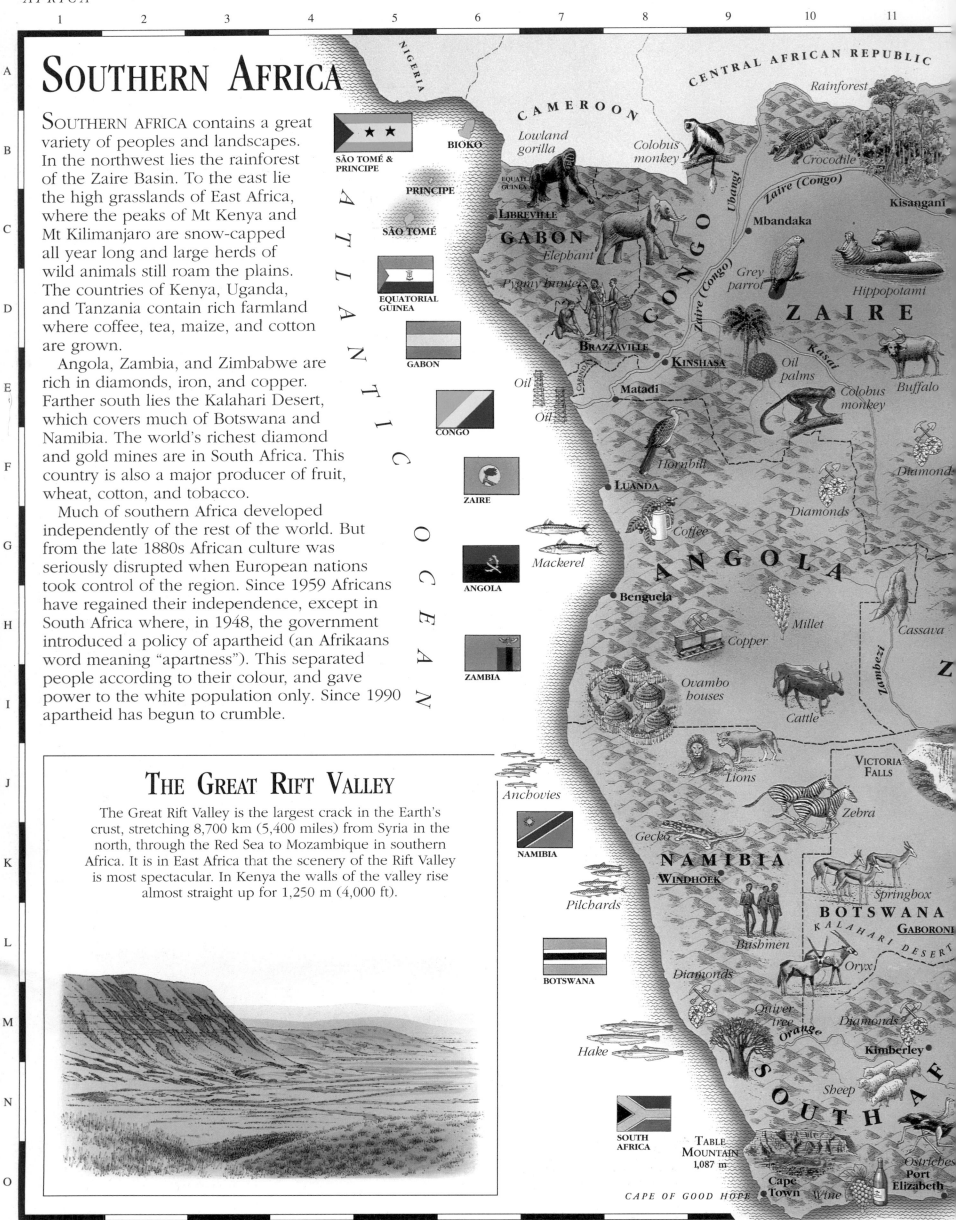

SÃO TOMÉ & PRINCIPE

EQUATORIAL GUINEA

GABON

CONGO

ZAIRE

ANGOLA

ZAMBIA

NAMIBIA

BOTSWANA

SOUTH AFRICA

NIGERIA
CAMEROON
CENTRAL AFRICAN REPUBLIC
Rainforest
Lowland gorilla
Colobus monkey
Crocodile
BIOKO
PRINCIPE
EQUAT. GUINEA
SÃO TOMÉ
LIBREVILLE
GABON
Zaire (Congo)
Ubangi
Kisangani
Mbandaka
Elephant
Grey parrot
ZAIRE
Hippopotami
Pygmy hunters
BRAZZAVILLE
KINSHASA
Oil palms
Kasai
Buffalo
Matadi
Colobus monkey
CABINDA
Oil
Oil
Diamond
ATLANTIC OCEAN
CONGO
LUANDA
Hornbill
Diamonds
Diamonds
Coffee
ANGOLA
Mackerel
Benguela
Millet
Cassava
Copper
Zambezi
Z
Ovambo houses
Cattle
VICTORIA FALLS
Lions
Anchovies
Zebra
Gecko
NAMIBIA
WINDHOEK
Springbox
Pilchards
BOTSWANA
NAMIBIA
Bushmen
KALAHARI DESERT
GABORONE
Oryx
Diamonds
Quiver tree
Orange
Diamonds
Hake
Kimberley
SOUTH AF
Sheep
SOUTH AFRICA
TABLE MOUNTAIN 1,087 m
Ostriches
Port Elizabeth
Cape Town
Wine
CAPE OF GOOD HOPE

SUDAN   **ETHIOPIA**   **SOMALIA**

UGANDA   **KENYA**

Elephant

Coffee

Giant groundsel

Gorilla

Gorilla

KAMPALA

Cotton

Mt Kenya 5,199 m

LAKE TURKANA

Cheetah

Lions

KIGALI

NAIROBI

Coffee

Coconut palms

Dhow

BUJUMBURA BURUNDI

Wildebeest

Chimpanzee

Masai herdsman

DODOMA

Kilimanjaro 5,896 m

Mombasa

Tourism

ZANZIBAR

Dar-es-Salaam

LAKE VICTORIA

GREAT RIFT VALLEY

LAKE TANGANYIKA

TANZANIA

Tea

Elephants

Leopard

Copper

Rhinoceros

Copper

Ndola

GREAT RIFT VALLEY

LAKE NYASA

Crested hornbill

Mangoes

ALDABRA ISLANDS

COMOROS

COMOROS

MAYOTTE (Fr)

MALAWI

LILONGWE

KARIBA DAM

Nacala

LUSAKA

Tea

Bananas

Ploughshare tortoise

Vanilla pods

LAKE KARIBA

ZIMBABWE

HARARE

Soapstone carving

Blantyre

Zambezi

Lemur

Long-tailed ground roller

Bulawayo

Beira

Bananas

ANTANANARIVO

MADAGASCAR

GREAT ZIMBABWE

MOZAMBIQUE CHANNEL

ZIMBABWE

Baobab tree

Black lemur

Limpopo

MOZAMBIQUE

Chameleon

Gold

Giraffes

Coelacanth

Cashew nuts

PRETORIA

Johannesburg

MAPUTO

MBABANE

Zulu

SWAZI LAND

Shrimps

Octopus tree

MADAGASCAR

AFRICA

MASERU

LESOTHO

Citrus fruits

SWAZILAND

Durban

Tourism

Umtata

LESOTHO

Pineapples   Lobster

INDIAN OCEAN

| 0 | 200 | 400 | 600 | 800 Kilometres |
| 0 | 100 | 200 | 300 | 400 | 500 Miles |

FACTS AND FIGURES

Zebra in the plains of Kenya. In recent years their numbers have been greatly reduced by hunting.

Highest mountains: Kilimanjaro (Tanzania), 5,896 m (19,344 ft); Mt Kenya (Kenya), 5,199 m (17,057 ft).

Longest rivers: Zaire, 4,667 km (2,900 miles); Zambezi, 2,756 km (1,700 miles).

Largest lakes: Lake Victoria, 69,400 sq km (26,800 sq miles); Lake Tanganyika, 32,900 sq km (13,860 sq miles).

Deepest lake: Lake Tanganyika, 1,435 m (4,708 ft).

Largest metropolitan areas: Kinshasa (Zaire), 2,796,000; Cape Town (South Africa), 2,350,200.

ANGOLA
Capital: Luanda

BOTSWANA
Capital: Gaborone

BURUNDI
Capital: Bujumbura

COMOROS
Capital: Moroni

CONGO
Capital: Brazzaville

EQUATORIAL GUINEA
Capital: Malabo

GABON
Capital: Libreville

KENYA
Capital: Nairobi

LESOTHO
Capital: Maseru

MADAGASCAR
Capital: Antananarivo

MALAWI
Capital: Lilongwe

MOZAMBIQUE
Capital: Maputo

NAMIBIA
Capital: Windhoek

RWANDA
Capital: Kigali

SÃO TOMÉ & PRINCIPE
Capital: São Tomé

SOUTH AFRICA
Capitals: Pretoria, Cape Town

SWAZILAND
Capital: Mbabane

TANZANIA
Capital: Dodoma

UGANDA
Capital: Kampala

ZAIRE
Capital: Kinshasa

ZAMBIA
Capital: Lusaka

ZIMBABWE
Capital: Harare

AUSTRALASIA

AUSTRALASIA, A REGION within Oceania, is named after Australia, the only large area of land it contains. Oceania consists of the world's smallest continent, Australia, the large islands of New Zealand, Papua New Guinea, and Fiji, and thousands of tiny islands scattered across the Pacific Ocean. Many of these islands are too small to be shown on the map below.

Australia, New Zealand and Papua New Guinea were once joined to Antarctica, but over millions of years they split off and drifted northwards across the Pacific Ocean. Because Oceania has been cut off from the other continents for so long, many of the plants and animals that have evolved there are found nowhere else in the world. The pouched mammals (marsupials) of Australia, such as the kangaroo, wallaby, and koala, and New Zealand's flightless birds, such as the kiwi and the kakapo, are examples of this.

One of the Fijian islands.

The Pacific islands have been formed in a number of ways. Some of them are the tips of mountains or volcanoes which rise up from the ocean bed. Others are formed of coral, created by the skeletons of millions of tiny sea creatures.

The Pacific islands fall into three groups, depending on their position in the ocean. In the middle of the Pacific

The city of Perth, Australia.

are the Polynesian islands, of which the biggest are the Hawaiian Islands. By the Stone Age, the light-skinned Polynesian people had become great explorers and navigators. They sailed all over the Pacific in their small double canoes, finding their way from the positions of the stars in the sky and the patterns of the waves. The Maori people of New Zealand are descended from Polynesians who settled there in about AD 900.

Maori carving, New Zealand.

The Micronesian islands are situated in the western Pacific. Like the Polynesians, the Micronesians were great seafarers, and traded throughout the region. The dark-skinned Melanesian people live on the islands closest to Australia and are related to Aboriginal Australians. Today, international tourism is a highly important industry in the Pacific islands, and this has brought many changes to the islanders' way of life.

Europeans, mainly from Britain and Ireland, began to settle in Australasia in the late 18th century and this pattern has continued. However, in recent times, the number of immigrants from other regions, particularly Asia, has increased markedly.

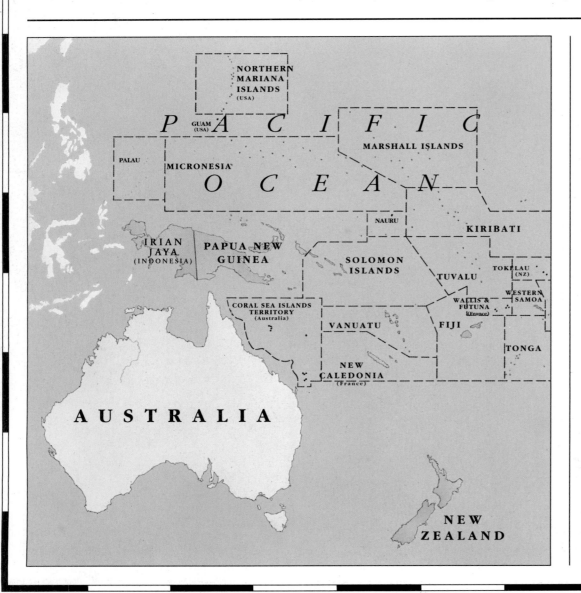

FACTS ABOUT AUSTRALASIA

Area: 8,923,000 sq km (3,445,197 sq miles). Australasia is a very small region that covers only six per cent of the total land area of the world.

Population: 27,531,000. Fewer people live in Australasia than in any other region, except Antarctica.

Number of independent countries: 14.

Largest country: Australia, 7,686,848 sq km (2,967,207 sq miles).

Most populated country: Australia, 17,800,000.

Largest metropolitan areas: Sydney (Australia), 3,698,500; Melbourne (Australia), 3,153,500; Brisbane (Australia), 1,327,000; Perth (Australia), 1,143,300; Adelaide (Australia), 1,023,700; Auckland (New Zealand), 966,300.

Highest mountains: Mt Wilhelm (Papua New Guinea), 4,509 m (14,793 ft); Mt Cook (New Zealand), 3,764 m (12,349 ft); Mt Kosciusko (Australia), 2,228 m (7,310 ft).

Longest river: Murray-Darling (Australia), 3,750 km (2,330 miles).

Largest deserts: Gibson Desert, Great Sandy Desert, Great Victoria Desert, Simpson Desert (all in Australia).

Largest islands: New Guinea, 808,510 sq km (312,168 sq miles); South Island, New Zealand, 150,460 sq km (58,080 sq miles).

Largest lakes: Lake Eyre (Australia), 9,583 sq km (3,700 sq miles); Lake Gairdner (Australia), 7,770 sq km (3,000 sq miles); Lake Torrens (Australia), 5,780 sq km (2,231 sq miles). Size varies according to the season. These are maximum areas.

Oldest rocks: The oldest rocks ever found on Earth are zircon crystals from the Jack Hills near Perth, Australia. They are 4,300 million years old.

A S I A

P A C I F I C

A
B
C
D

M I C R O N E S I A

MARIANAS

MARSHALL
ISLANDS

HAWAIIAN ISLANDS

CAROLINE ISLANDS

M E L A N E S I A

NAURU

KIRIBATI

NEW GUINEA
Mt
WILHELM △
4,509 m

NEW
IRELAND

NEW BRITAIN

SOLOMON ISLANDS

TUVALU

ARAFURA
SEA

TIMOR
SEA

O C E A N

GULF OF
CARPENTARIA

C O R A L
SEA

VANUATU

WESTERN
SAMOA

KIMBERLEY
PLATEAU

GREAT
SANDY
DESERT

A U S T R A L I A

MACDONNELL
RANGES

NEW
CALEDONIA

FIJI

P O L Y N E S I A

Gascoyne

GIBSON
DESERT

SIMPSON
DESERT

GREAT DIVIDING RANGE

TONGA

GREAT VICTORIA
DESERT

LAKE
EYRE

NULLARBOR
PLAIN

LAKE
GAIRDNER

LAKE
TORRENS

Darling

GREAT AUSTRALIAN BIGHT

Murray

Mt KOSCIUSKO △
2,228 m

T A S M A N
SEA

TASMANIA

NEW ZEALAND
△ Mt COOK
3,764 m

L

M

N

S O U T H E R N   O C E A N

A N T A R C T I C A

O

AUSTRALIA

AUSTRALIA is a country and a continent. It is almost as big as the United States. Much of the country is hot and dry, especially in the middle where there are deserts. Few people live in these dry areas, but there are large sheep and cattle farms called "stations" and some mining. East of the hills and mountains of the Great Dividing Range and on the island of Tasmania the climate is wetter, and it is here that most people live. Two-thirds of all Australians live in the small number of large cities, particularly the state capitals, such as Sydney, Melbourne, and Brisbane. The population of Australia is only 17.6 million people, compared with 245 million in the United States.

Millions of years ago, Australia drifted away from the other continents of the world. As a result, many of the plants and animals which evolved there are not found anywhere else in the world. Many of the mammals, such as kangaroos and wombats, are marsupials, which rear their young in pouches on their stomachs.

The first inhabitants of Australia arrived about 100,000 years ago and Aboriginal Australians are their descendants. Europeans did not settle in Australia until 200 years ago. Since 1945 the population has doubled, with people coming to Australia from many parts of the world.

THE GREAT BARRIER REEF

The Great Barrier Reef is a maze of about 2,500 coral reefs and islands stretching 2,000 km (1,200 miles) along the coast of Queensland. It contains over 300 different species of coral and thousands of fish. Coral is formed by millions of tiny sea animals called polyps, which cement themselves together. The Great Barrier Reef is slowly being eaten away by creatures called crown-of-thorns starfish. In order to protect the reef from further destruction by both humans and natural causes, the Great Barrier Reef Marine Park has been formed.

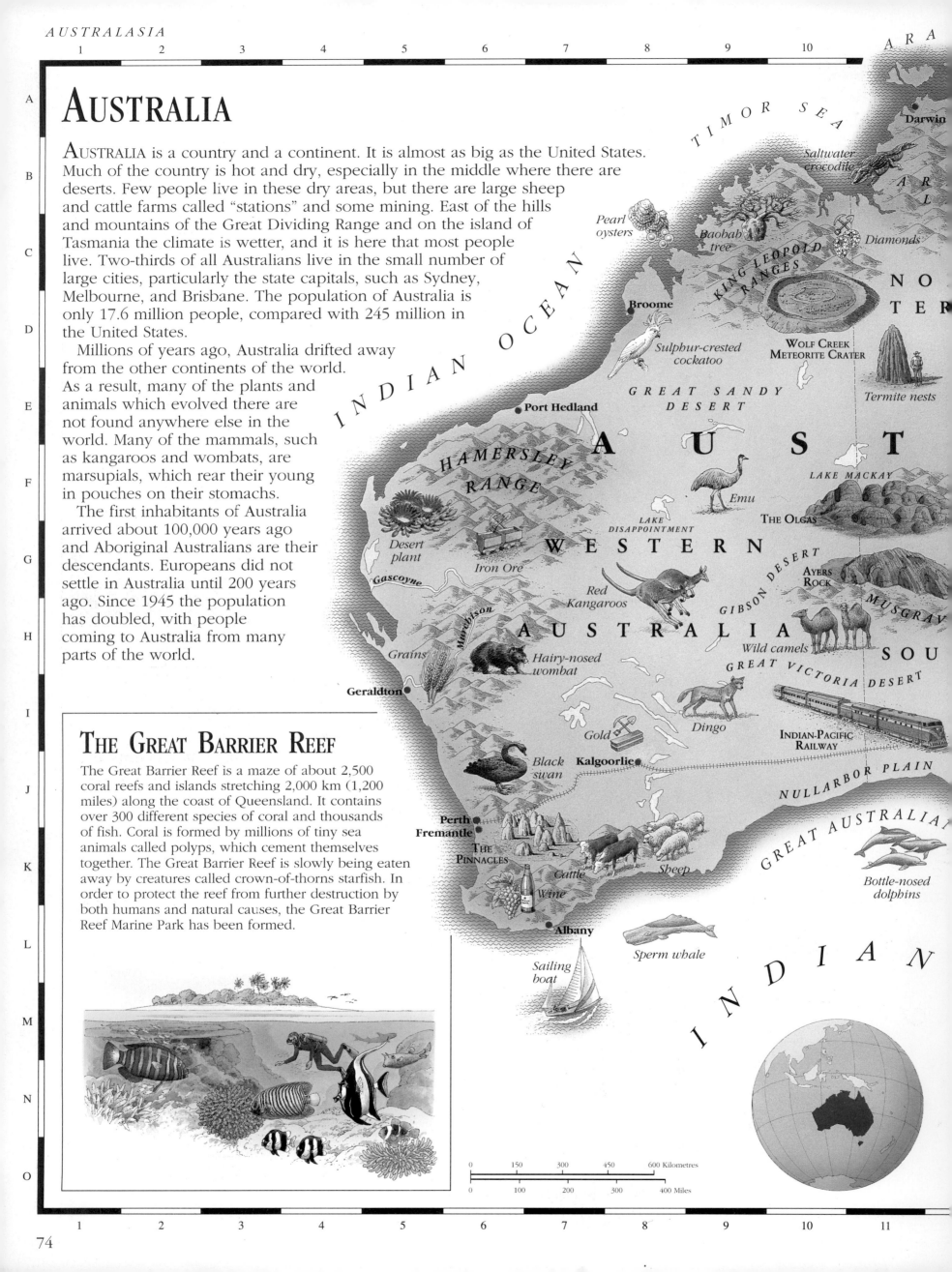

TIMOR SEA

Darwin

Saltwater crocodile

Pearl oysters

Baobab tree

Diamonds

KING LEOPOLD RANGES

Broome

INDIAN OCEAN

Sulphur-crested cockatoo

WOLF CREEK METEORITE CRATER

NO TER

GREAT SANDY DESERT

Termite nests

Port Hedland

AUST

HAMERSLEY RANGE

Emu

LAKE MACKAY

Desert plant

LAKE DISAPPOINTMENT

THE OLGAS

WESTERN

Iron Ore

Gascoyne

Red Kangaroos

GIBSON DESERT

AYERS ROCK

MUSGRAV

Murchison

Grains

AUSTRALIA

Wild camels

SOU

Hairy-nosed wombat

GREAT VICTORIA DESERT

Geraldton

Gold

Dingo

INDIAN-PACIFIC RAILWAY

Black swan

Kalgoorlie

NULLARBOR PLAIN

Perth
Fremantle

THE PINNACLES

GREAT AUSTRALIA

Cattle

Sheep

Bottle-nosed dolphins

Wine

Albany

Sperm whale

INDIAN

Sailing boat

0	150	300	450	600 Kilometres
0	100	200	300	400 Miles

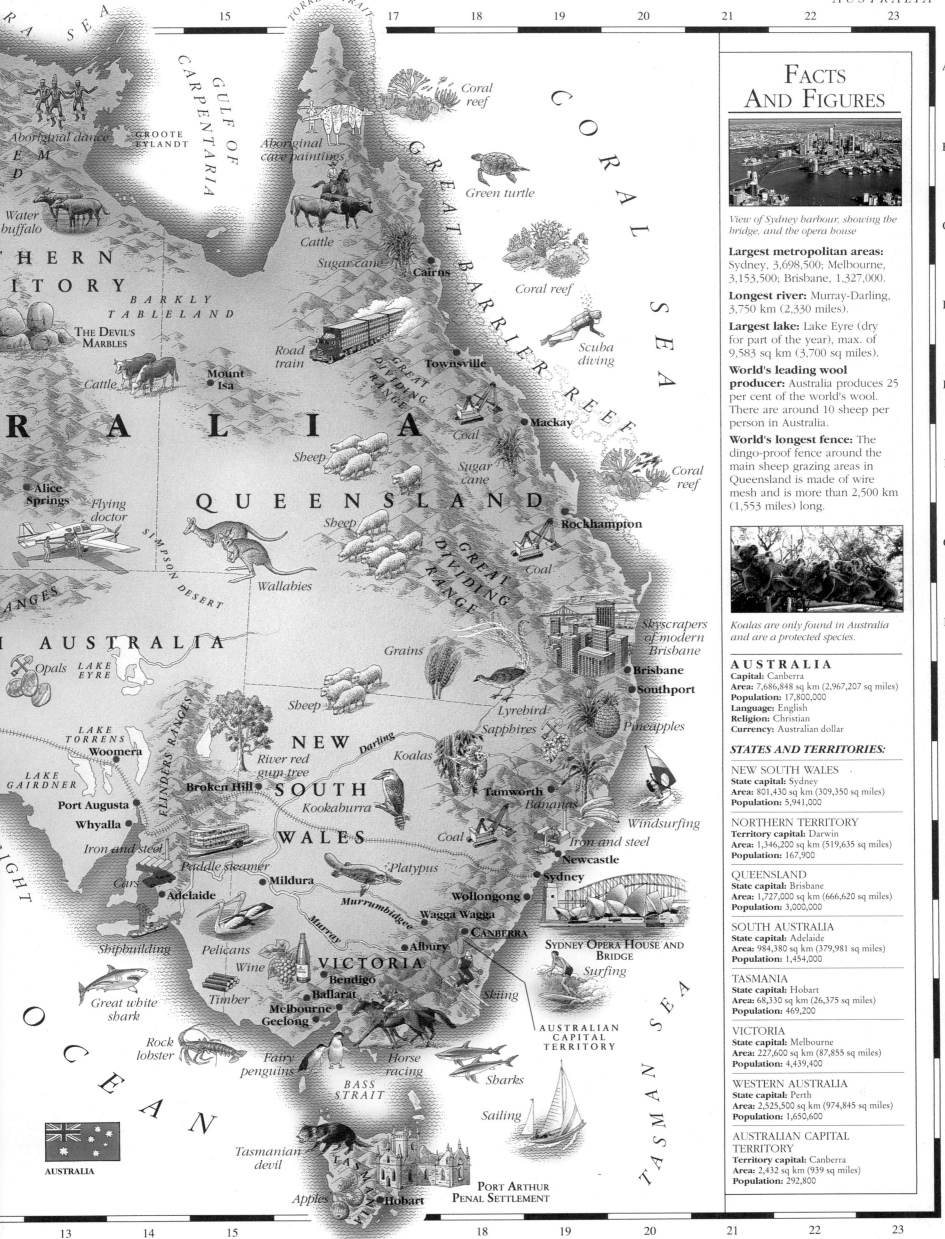

FACTS AND FIGURES

View of Sydney harbour, showing the bridge, and the opera house.

Largest metropolitan areas: Sydney, 3,698,500; Melbourne, 3,153,500; Brisbane, 1,327,000.

Longest river: Murray-Darling, 3,750 km (2,330 miles).

Largest lake: Lake Eyre (dry for part of the year), max. of 9,583 sq km (3,700 sq miles).

World's leading wool producer: Australia produces 25 per cent of the world's wool. There are around 10 sheep per person in Australia.

World's longest fence: The dingo-proof fence around the main sheep grazing areas in Queensland is made of wire mesh and is more than 2,500 km (1,553 miles) long.

Koalas are only found in Australia and are a protected species.

AUSTRALIA
Capital: Canberra
Area: 7,686,848 sq km (2,967,207 sq miles)
Population: 17,800,000
Language: English
Religion: Christian
Currency: Australian dollar

STATES AND TERRITORIES:

NEW SOUTH WALES
State capital: Sydney
Area: 801,430 sq km (309,350 sq miles)
Population: 5,941,000

NORTHERN TERRITORY
Territory capital: Darwin
Area: 1,346,200 sq km (519,635 sq miles)
Population: 167,900

QUEENSLAND
State capital: Brisbane
Area: 1,727,000 sq km (666,620 sq miles)
Population: 3,000,000

SOUTH AUSTRALIA
State capital: Adelaide
Area: 984,380 sq km (379,981 sq miles)
Population: 1,454,000

TASMANIA
State capital: Hobart
Area: 68,330 sq km (26,375 sq miles)
Population: 469,200

VICTORIA
State capital: Melbourne
Area: 227,600 sq km (87,855 sq miles)
Population: 4,439,400

WESTERN AUSTRALIA
State capital: Perth
Area: 2,525,500 sq km (974,845 sq miles)
Population: 1,650,600

AUSTRALIAN CAPITAL TERRITORY
Territory capital: Canberra
Area: 2,432 sq km (939 sq miles)
Population: 292,800

NEW ZEALAND

NEW ZEALAND lies in the Pacific Ocean, about 1,600 km (1,000 miles) southeast of Australia. The country is made up of two main islands: the North Island and the South Island. Most people live on the North Island, which has a warm, tropical climate.

The first people to reach New Zealand were the Maoris, who started to settle there around AD 900. They sailed to New Zealand from the Polynesia islands in small, open boats. The first European to sight the country was the Dutch explorer, Abel Tasman, in 1642. New Zealand became a British colony in 1840 and an independent country in 1907.

Today the population is a mixture of Maoris and people of British descent. The country's wealth comes from industry and farming, particularly raising cattle and sheep. New Zealand is the world's biggest exporter of lamb and second largest exporter of dairy products.

HOT SPRINGS

In the region around Rotorua, on the North Island, hot water bubbles out of the ground. In some places there is such pressure underground that water is forced out in a jet called a geyser, reaching heights of up to 70 m (230 ft). The steam produced in this area is used to drive electric power stations.

Map labels

Oysters
Tourism
Kauri pine
Snapper
Whangarei

HAURAKI GULF
Auckland
Sailing
Iron and steel
Windsurfing
Dairy cattle
BAY OF PLENTY

NORTH ISLAND
Hamilton
Tauranga
Rotorua
Maori carving
Kiwi fruit
Waikato
LAKE TAUPO
MT TARANAKI (MT EGMONT) 2,518 m
Gisborne
Oil and gas
New Plymouth
Haka (Maori dance)
HAWKE BAY
Napier
Wanganui
Hastings
Snapper
Palmerston North
Gannets

TASMAN BAY
COOK STRAIT
Nelson
Blenheim
WELLINGTON
PARLIAMENT BUILDINGS (WELLINGTON)

NEW ZEALAND

Apples
Kiwi
Greymouth
Sheep
Kaikoura
Sperm whale

NEW ZEALAND

TASMAN SEA
MT COOK 3,764 m
SOUTH ISLAND
SOUTHERN ALPS
CHRISTCHURCH CATHEDRAL
Christchurch
CANTERBURY PLAINS
Textiles
Takahe
MILFORD SOUND
Skiing
Timaru
Tarakihi
Sheep
Royal albatross
Kakapo
Apricots
Dunedin
Rugby
Invercargill
FOVEAUX STRAIT
Rock lobster
STEWART ISLAND

PACIFIC OCEAN

Scale: 0 50 100 150 200 250 Kilometres
0 50 100 150 Miles

FACTS AND FIGURES

The city of Auckland lies between Waitemata and Manukau Harbours and is a centre for water sports.

NEW ZEALAND

Capital: Wellington
Area: 268,676 sq km (103,736 sq miles)
Population: 3,500,000
Languages: English, Maori
Religion: Christian
Currency: New Zealand dollar
Government: Monarchy

Largest lake: Lake Taupo, 606 sq km (234 sq miles).

Longest river: Waikato, 425 km (264 miles).

Largest cities: Auckland, 966,300; Wellington, 404,200; Christchurch, 308,200.

Long inlets of sea cut into the land on the southwestern coast of the South Island. The area is called Fiordland, after the Norwegian fjords.

INDEX

This index contains the names of places shown on continental and country maps. The page number is given in bold type after the place name. The grid reference follows in lighter type (see also page 13, How to Use This Atlas).

ACKNOWLEDGMENTS

Dorling Kindersley would like to thank the following:
Kate Woodward and Anna Kunst for research, Chris Scollen and Richard Czapnik for additional design help, and Struan Reid for editorial assistance.

Picture Research Cynthia Hole

Political Maps Luciano Corbella

Picture credits
(r = right, l = left, t = top, c = centre, b = bottom)

Australian Overseas Information Service, London 75tr, 75br
Australian Tourist Commission, London 72tr

de Beers 66tr
Charles Bowman 16br, 25tr, 34c, 51tr, 51tl, 52tl, 59tr, 59br, 76tl,
Canadian High Commission 16tc, 19tc
Caribbean Tourist Office 27r
The J. Allan Cash Photolibrary 6tr, 6bl, 12tl, 12br, 20l, 23br, 23bl, 36tl, 36br, 45tl, 76br,
Lester Cheeseman 52bc, 65tl, 65tr, 65bc, 66tr
Chilean Embassy 33br, 33bl
Chinese Tourist Office 63br
Bruce Coleman Ltd / Fritz Prenzel 7cl,
Commission of the European Communities 34tl
Susan Cunningham 31br
Richard Czapnik 66c
Egyptian Tourist Office 57tr, 69tr

Chris Fairclough Colour Library 12c, 21tr, 43tr, 43br, 45c, 52tr, 72c, 72bl,
Fiat Press Office 46cr
French Railways Ltd 39cr
Susan Griggs Agency / Rob Cousins 7tl; George Hall 12tr
Robert Harding Picture Library 6tl
Hutchison Library / John Dowman 6br; Anwa Tully 12bl
The Image Bank / Guido Rossi 12bc
Italian State Tourist Office 46tl
Kenyan Tourist Office 71tr
Anna Kunst 55tr, 55cr
Keith Lye 16cl, 28tl, 28bc, 52tr, 57br, 63tr
Hugo Maertens 41br

Norwegian Tourist Office 14tr, 15tr
Peruvian Embassy 28tr, 31tr
Roger Priddy 34tr, 36tr, 39tr, 39br, 46cl
South American Pictures 33tl
Spanish National Tourist Office 49tr
The Telegraph Colour Library 41bl
Travel Photo International 7tr, 7cr, 41tr, 43cr, 45br, 49br
Zefa Picture Library 12cr
Zentrale Farbbild Agentur / D. Frobisch 7br

Every effort has been made to trace the copyright holders and we apologise in advance for any unintentional omissions. We would be pleased to insert the appropriate acknowledgment in any subsequent edition of this book.